MARKET GARDENING

MARKET GARDENING
Growing and Selling Produce

Ric Staines

Fulcrum Publishing
Golden, Colorado

First published in 1990 by The Crowood Press
Ramsbury, Marlborough, Wiltshire, England SN 8 2HE
All rights reserved.

Library of Congress Cataloging-in-Publication Data
Staines, Ric.
    Market gardening / Ric Staines.
        p.   cm.
    Includes bibliographical references and index.
    ISBN 1-55591-100-5
    1. Truck farming. 2. Fruit-culture. 3. Truck farming—United
States. 4. Fruit-culture—United States. 5. Vegetables—Marketing.
6. Fruit—Marketing. 7. Vegetables—United States—Marketing.
8. Fruit—United States—Marketing. I. Title.
SB321.S66 1991
635—dc20   91-71363
                                                    CIP

Printed in the United States of America

9   8   7   6   5   4   3   2   1

Fulcrum Publishing
350 Indiana Street
Golden, Colorado 80401

This book is dedicated to
all who make a living
from the soil

CONTENTS

Acknowledgments / ix

Introduction / xi

Chapter 1
Market Gardening Today / 1

Chapter 2
Marketing / 9

Chapter 3
How to Grow: Soils and Their Management / 27

Chapter 4
Crop Requirements and Nutrition / 45

Chapter 5
Cropping Possibilities / 61

Chapter 6
Machinery and Equipment / 93

Chapter 7
Protective Structures and Films / 111

Chapter 8
Pest, Disease and Weed Control / 123

Chapter 9
Management / 139

Appendix 1
Liming Materials / 147

Appendix 2
U.S. Measure and Metric Measure Conversion Chart / 149

Appendix 3
Associations / 151

Bibliography / 153

Index / 155

ACKNOWLEDGMENTS

I would like to thank all those who have helped me in writing this book, especially my colleagues at Otley College, the students, my parents who gave me an interest in horticulture and last, but not least, my long-suffering wife and children without whose help, encouragement and typing it would not have been possible. I would also like to thank Otley College and the following people for allowing me to photograph their holdings, farm shops, etc.: J. Coles of Roseleigh Nurseries, Kirton, J. Craig of Nature's Foods, Little Bardford, R. Blyth of Friday Street Farm Shop, Farnham, Saxmundham and A. Simpson of Hillside Nurseries, Hintlesham.

In the United States, a special thank you goes out to the various vendors of the Boulder Farmers Market.

*M*arket gardening. What do I mean by market gardening? When I put this question to a colleague he said, "There's no such thing now."

"Yes there is," I replied, "it's ... it's ... well, you know, a market garden." These two words hold a lot of meaning, much more than just "gardening for a market." For this is really how it all started, with people selling off surplus produce from their gardens for a little extra. As towns such as London grew bigger, a steady market for fresh food developed.

Market gardening in England began in the sixteenth century. The charter of the Gardeners' Company and the Fruiterers' Company was granted in 1605. It was said that a holding of three acres could keep a man and his family and employ outside labor. In 1750 bell-glass cloches and garden frames were being used and produce was being grown and sold directly to the public close to roads. Was this the birth of the farm shop? The market garden grew from these beginnings. Always just outside the town and moving out as the town moved out, market gardeners provided a range of vegetables, fruit and flowers to town and, later, to city dwellers. The range increased as new types were introduced from abroad and gained acceptance with the buying public. This development has continued right up to the present day. We tend to think market gardening has died out because new terms have appeared: smallholding, self-sufficiency, etc. These are really trying to describe something different.

The development of produce to consumer sales has developed over the last two hundred years, in similar fashion to the Great Britain experience. In recent years, the disadvantages of hauling produce long distances have made locally grown and sold produce more attractive.

In the United States, almost every major city can boast of one or more farmers market, local access to farm shops and pick-your-own gardens. Rural areas—even those great distances from large towns and cities—have flea markets where producers set up vegetable stands.

So what is a market garden? By tradition, it is a smallholding of up to ten acres producing a range of crops such as vegetables, fruit and possibly a few flowers. Modern influences have changed this, as I hope this book will show.

The book will also give the reader a good understanding of the principles of growing crops commercially in this day and age. It is not a blueprint for how to grow certain crops, but covers a comprehensive range of factors to ensure that anyone in or thinking of taking up market gardening will stand a better chance of success. Good luck to you.

CHAPTER 1

Market Gardening Today

*T*he modern market garden holding is very different from its predecessors. This is due in no small part to the many modern developments within the horticultural industry. Improved varieties of seed, methods of propagation and g rowing and the advances made in plant nutrition have all had their impact. So too has the change in the traditional outlets for the produce from the market garden. Both the buying and the eating habits of the public have changed dramatically over the last twenty-five years. In this ever-changing world the market garden has had advantages. It is perhaps easier for small producers to alter or adapt their ways. More recently, the changes in the way consumers buy their fresh produce have made life both easier and more difficult. The advent of supermarkets has made it virtually impossible for small growers to supply them. This, coupled with the reduction in the number and importance of local wholesale markets, has meant changes to the outlets for market gardens. Some have found success specializing in certain crops, particularly those crops that require a high degree of skill and labor, and so are not as profitable for the bigger growers to produce. The profit markets on crops such as lettuce have not risen in real terms for at least the past ten years so the grower either has to become more and more efficient and increase levels of production or find a more profitable line. All these factors combined have helped to make the market gardener specialize.

More recently, the interest in whole foods, limited-process foods and organically produced foods, and the advent of farmers markets, farm shops and pick-your-own gardens have revitalized the market garden. Farmers markets and farm shops grew out of a need for the small producer to maximize his or her returns by cutting out the middlemen. Development has now virtually turned full circle in the case of farm shops that have really come out of town shops, not large and supplying everything but specializing in fresh local produce. Some also supply imported produce such as oranges and bananas and even more exotic fruit because this became a natural extension of the business. Pick-your-own gardens developed alongside this as no harvesting labor was required—the customers did it themselves.

More recently again, the swing in public attitudes to care for the environment and to move away from a prepackaged lifestyle should go far in aiding a resurgence in market gardening. Perhaps the fastest growing sector at present is that of organic production. The demand for produce grown without the use of chemicals in a way that cannot harm the environment far exceeds current production. This is one option to which any market gardener must give serious consideration. With this development the history of market gardening has completed a full cycle by returning to its roots (no pun intended). Becoming a fully fledged organic grower may necessitate a total rethinking of the way crops are grown and handled and growing lands are nurtured. It is something that should not be taken on halfheartedly but can be made to work. I know of one holding in central Michigan that has been producing organically both outdoors and under glass for many years. They do not even ask a premium on the price of their produce.

Nearer to my home in East Anglia, England, there is a market garden that decided to convert to organics about three years ago. The grower expected many problems, especially with pests and diseases, but has found that his fears were totally unfounded. The demand for his produce has grown and he only wishes he made the change earlier. Perhaps the biggest problems the modern organic movement have are its image and the fact that those involved cannot agree on what exactly constitutes "organic."

In the United States, both state and federal governmental agencies have begun establishing criteria for organically grown produce. The U.S. Department of Agriculture has been given the task of developing the National Organic Standards Board (NOSB), autho-

A modern market garden.

rized by the 1990 Farm Bill.

The purpose of the act is to establish a national standard governing the marketing of certain agricultural products as organically produced products, and to facilitate interstate commerce in fresh and processed food that is organically produced. A certification program will be developed to ensure that produce marketed as "certified organic" meets minimum production standards. The NOSB is authorized by the 1990 Farm Bill to begin in 1993, but as yet no funding has been allocated to establish the program.

A number of states, however, have taken it upon themselves to establish "certified organic" label programs. Colorado is now one of seventeen states to enact legislation that regulates the organic produce industry.

The Colorado Organic Certification Act of 1989 defines the term organic and specifies conditions under which so designated products must be grown. In addition, it gives the state department of agriculture the authority to oversee an organic certification program.

In states where certified organic programs do not exist, everyone could call their produce organic.

There are variations in state legislation, but generally organic is defined as agricultural products grown or produced without the use of synthetic pesticides, synthetically compounded fertilizers or synthetic growth hormones. Legislation usually prohibits the use of pesticides, plant regulators (ingredients that can change the growth rate of plants), defoliants and desiccants (ingredients that artificially increase the drying time of plant tissue), and describes the use of biological control.

Under most state legislation, produce can be certified organic only if it has been grown in soil or a growth medium free of synthetic pesticides for a certain period of time.

The programs are voluntary on the part of the producer. If a producer is selling under a certified organic seal, it means the produce and fields where the produce was grown have been inspected and meet the qualifications of the legislation.

Selling cut flowers, houseplants and bedding plants are also viable products for the ambitious market gardener.

Roadside stands are popular in many parts of the United States.

Of course, it is still possible for producers to call their produce organic without being part of the certified program. If you are in doubt as to your state requirement, call your state department of agriculture for more information and keep abreast of the developments of the national NOSB program.

Many modern market gardeners may fall in a halfway category: They may not be able to afford or want to use the vast array of modern chemicals, but they are not totally committed to the organic movement. They do, however, have certain marketing advantages, such as freshness and the fact that they are local; these should be fully exploited to make the business successful.

Life has recently been made much easier. The range of machinery and equipment available now has enabled the modern market gardener to utilize his or her skills to the fullest. Sitting on a tractor or planting machine may at times be hard work but does leave the grower with more time and energy to devote to other jobs that put the finishing touches on his or her product. The modern pedestrian-operated Rototiller and the small or compact tractor are ideal tools; they can do a wide range of tasks and save time and energy. There is also a wide range of other growing aids. The development of modern floating films and poly-tunnels has reduced the amount of easily breakable glass on holdings. Gone are the days of glass cloches and the care that handling them involved. Now tunnels and rivers or lakes or floating film have replaced them.

The advantages in plant nutrition and pest and disease control have all contributed to make the modern market garden. Developments in plant breeding and new and improved strains have increased yields beyond all recognition.

The modern market garden is not all muck and mystery, but a modern, highly efficient agribusiness, producing a high-quality product to satisfy a changing local demand.

CHAPTER 2

Marketing

 arketing is often forgotten when a new market garden venture is set up. Yet it can make or break the developing business. A well-devised marketing strategy can give the business a much greater chance of success right from the start; it is far better than forming a marketing strategy out of necessity over a number of years. This is not to say that the strategy should be inflexible. Having a definite strategy to start with allows one to start at a known position, then to take all outside influences into account before changing the policy.

Do not grow and then think, "Where can I sell this?" Grow for one or more outlets. This is the most important single point for success. For those considering a new business this may appear to be a difficult thing to do but, like all aspects of a new business, good planning and forethought are worth their weight in good returns.

For example, imagine you have found what seems to be the ideal holding—cheap, southern exposure, deep fertile soil, natural water supply, etc.—and it is thirty-five miles from the nearest large town. Closer than that are perhaps three towns, four farm shops and another market garden. Having planned a good production for the first season of growing on your new eight-acre holding, you have lots of produce ready to sell. Then what? The local shops already have their suppliers, the nearest market is thirty-five miles away. You line up a good outlet that wants three deliveries a week—not a large amount at first, but with potential. Now let's look at this more closely with three trips per week to this outlet: three round trips, i.e., 3 x 70 miles = 210 miles; vehicle returns, 25 mpg = 8.4 gallons of fuel.

This works out at current prices to approximately $3.50 per trip, plus the cost of the time it takes to make a seventy-mile round trip

Selling produce right on your property is ideal for many, especially if the location is easy to access and has enough passersby to bring in newcomers.

and the cost of operating a vehicle. At a very low estimate, this adds up to $14.00 per trip. What is the profit margin on the trip? If it is a small delivery it could be less than $14.00, so delivery or transport can obviously play a vital role in the profitability of the business.

What other sales possibilities are there? Local outlets? Are they big enough and can you break in on existing suppliers? A farm shop? There are four in the area already and probably only one good one, but it is thirty-five miles away from a main center of population. Are you on a main road? What other attractions are there in the area? There will possibly not be enough customers to rely on. Perhaps the five-acre holding with a house only five miles from the town may have been a better buy after all.

Is all this just hypothesis? I'm afraid not. The type of holding and its location in relation to a proposed market is of paramount importance. Soil fertility can be improved, but costs of transportation

A traditional farm shop.

and marketing costs cannot—they always go up. Location is also of paramount importance when considering a farm shop enterprise or a pick-your-own garden. If the holding is not to be the main source of income, then the proximity to markets may not be of such importance, but it will still have a substantial effect on the viability and profitability of the venture. If you have already purchased your holding this may influence considerably what and how you grow.

This is an appropriate time to consider what the potential outlets are. Obviously they will relate to the types of crops you are growing or plan to grow. Basically, these outlets can be subdivided to on-farm and off-farm outlets. So let's now see what the possibilities are.

ON-FARM OUTLETS

Farm Shops

These can have many advantages such as no transportation and packaging costs, everything is under your own control and the maximum price is achieved for the products since no middlemen are involved. The disadvantages may include the wide range of crops that need to be grown. Location is important (it will need to be near a center of population or have good passing trade—preferably both), as are good road access and a parking area. The local competition will also need to be considered. What are the planning requirements? (See Chapter 9, page 140.) Permission may be required if you sell produce not grown by you. Also, it may be difficult to obtain staff.

Farm shops are often associated with pick-your-own enterprises. These two types of outlet do seem to complement each other, but is your holding big enough and is it situated near a large center of population?

Pick Your Own

These enterprises lend themselves to soft fruit and a range of vegetables such as peas, beans, sweet corn, peppers, etc. As with farm shops, location will play a vital role in the success of the enterprise, as will the organization of your own resources. A suitable cash point is required, good signposting, etc. Security should be high on your list of priorities, as should be a good car parking area. Do you need to consider other facilities such as toilets, picnic area, children's play area, etc.? Also, liability insurance questions should be discussed with a professional.

Pick-your-own enterprises by their very nature have a seasonal bias and this can cause problems for a sole-income business with regard to the annual cash flow.

It may be possible with both of these types of enterprise to widen the range of products being offered and help to complement their seasonal nature by extending the season or filling in quiet times with pot plants, bedding plants and even nursery stock, especially container-grown herbs, shrubs and trees. A number of modern garden centers now sell vegetables and fruit, so it may be time to take a leaf out of their book, so to speak, and sell plants as well.

This popular local farmers market specializes in providing country-fresh produce to an urban community.

OFF-FARM OUTLETS

Local Farmers Markets

Taking a stall in a farmers market still allows the grower a certain amount of control so it may be a useful outlet for produce. But several factors need to be considered: Is there available staff to run the stall? Is any staff required back at the holding? Will you be able to resupply the stall on busy days or does distance and lack of staff make this impossible? As a second outlet this option may work well, enabling the grower to reduce surpluses and yet retain the maximum price for his or her product, for yet again, like both the farm shop and pick-your-own garden, no middlemen are involved. Such a stall will also reduce the costs of packages since boxes can be reused.

To work successfully it requires a reasonable range of products displayed regularly, which could cause problems with cropping schedules. Also, depending on the day of the week, it may mean a reduced volume of produce is available the following day. This could be a problem if the market happens to be on a Friday, and Saturday is your

Flea markets provide a similar service to both the produce seller and the buyer as do farmers markets.

busy day in the farm shop. Which is it to be—is it more acceptable to run out in the stall or in the shop? This would be an option worth investigating before finally settling on a marketing strategy.

If the farmers market stall is your only or primary marketing avenue, be sure to check with the market organizers and your state and local sales tax office for requirements of sales tax collection.

Flea Markets

Most cities and larger towns across the United States have developed weekend flea markets. A favorite among the regular shoppers are the fresh produce stands. These stands usually specialize in locally grown produce and plants.

The same marketing techniques applied to a farmers market stall apply to a flea market stand. Location, availability of personnel and sales are all important factors. In addition, consider using a flea market stand all year. Most markets are open every weekend throughout the year, with some open on Wednesday through the warmer months.

Most flea markets offer discounted booth space and premium locations for those reserving the space on an extended lease. This may be an attractive marketing opportunity for many market gardeners. By leasing the space, you will pay less in the long run and repeat customers will be able to find you and your produce easily.

Sales tax issues are a consideration for any vendor. Check with the market for sales tax requirements. It may be possible to pay the market itself the sales tax requirements, thus eliminating the need to obtain an individual sales tax license.

Local Retailers

Now we have to go a little farther away from home to the local retailer. Here again regular supplies are required. It should be possible to build up a good personal relationship with the retailer; establishing good communication helps considerably. The volume of product taken may vary from retailer to retailer, and this may cause transportation problems as in the example earlier in this chapter. Assuming they are within economic distance, however, local retailers may be a good outlet as it enables you to get on with the growing and keeps you away from the general public!

Prices received from the local retailer should be above those quoted as market wholesale prices. Regular checking in trade magazines and local newspapers will ensure prices are realistic.

The local retailer also benefits by getting a fresher product from a locally known supplier. To achieve this, you the grower need to remember that in harvest quality and grading you are competing with the "big boys," but you have freshness and adaptability (adjusting grading and crop requirements to retailers' requirements) on your side. With a little effort, a good working relationship can be achieved to the mutual benefit of both parties.

Catering Establishments

These still retain the local flavor or may in fact be looking for local flavor. They may have general requirements for good quality produce but could have very specific requirements, for example, courgettes with the flowers still attached. There have been several notable cases of growers finding that the catering establishments in their area could not obtain a range of products and so set out to satisfy their demand. To do this successfully one has to work closely with the chef concerned and pay great attention to detail in the crop husbandry. When involved in this specialized market a very high return is required for such specialized crops, although it may only be a case of leaving a few inches of stalk on the young carrots or some other such criterion that would normally cause the produce to be of an inferior grade according to statutory standards. The viability of such specialized growing depends on sufficient demand; being close to an area where there are several upscale hotels or restaurants will obviously help. Another possibility is so-called exotic vegetables for diverse culinary tastes, including ethnic specialties. These could range from peppers to Chinese leaves to fresh spices. These could then be sold to restaurants and other ethnic and gourmet food shops.

Local Wholesalers

These are sometimes referred to as secondary wholesalers but they can be considered as one and the same. Their main business is procuring produce to supply a large number of local retailers, restaurants and hotels with a full range of produce. They produce these supplies from local growers and the major wholesale markets. They are, if you like, the ubiquitous middlemen. As such, though, they can serve a very useful purpose.

These local wholesalers can be a major outlet for your produce they can often handle relatively large volumes of product. Even so, to gain the best from them for both price and service it is best to build up a good relationship with them. This is best done by good communication and a regular supply of quality product. If this local wholesaler knows he or she gets regular product from you, the wholesaler is much more likely to help if you have an unexpected oversupply of one crop. Also, if your quality is always high and the wholesaler knows the bottom boxes are as good as the top, he or she is much more likely to take your product in times of oversupply rather than that of someone else who occasionally supplies surplus product of indifferent quality. It is consistency, quality and communication that achieve the best prices and service.

I have not yet said much in detail about communication, though I have mentioned it in passing several times. What do I mean by this? Well, it really ties in with the other two criteria: consistency and quality. If, for example, you normally supply the wholesaler with fifty boxes of, say, lettuce on Thursday and something happened to the crop such as mildew, or the goat got out on Tuesday, let him or her know that you can only supply twenty-five boxes on Wednesday, or as soon as possible, rather than waiting until the wholesaler turns up to collect the product. If the latter occurs, it may mean the wholesaler has to let down his or her own customers, something that might be taken out on you! If you have let the wholesaler know in good time, he or she can make alternative arrangements and find other suppliers or warn customers. This all helps to build trust and mutual respect. The same is true with regard to quality as well. It also does not hurt to ask regularly about prices and other market trends, volume of supply, new products, etc.

Although the prices returned by such people are not necessarily the best, they have to make a living and run the costly transport. I would suggest that every grower be on good terms with at least one local wholesaler—even if the volume the wholesaler may actually take is small, it can be worth every penny if the volume you have is too large for your other outlets to take but too small for delivery to a major market.

If you do have a good relationship with a local wholesaler who makes regular calls to the major markets, he or she may deliver your produce there at a very reasonable price; the truck may well be travelling empty to Kansas City or New York to collect oranges or bananas; to get some money for the empty trips is obviously worthwhile. So if you want to get produce to the major wholesalers, this may be an economical way of doing so.

Major Regional Markets

These are major regional markets such as Green Market in Brooklyn and others in cities such as New York, Chicago, Kansas City, Los Angeles, Miami, etc., around the rest of the country. The demands of these markets for continuity and quality are similar to the local wholesaler, and building a good relationship may be even more important since almost all contact will be over the phone and a personal touch may be difficult to achieve. In addition, quantity is a major consideration. The amount of time and expense involved in reaching this market tends to dictate the necessity of large quantities.

It can also be time-consuming to deliver produce to them. Most markets open about 4 A.M. or earlier, with most sales occurring at around 6 A.M., and they are relatively quiet by 8 A.M. So produce will need to be delivered in the early hours of the morning and you may not get home until late morning. Getting up at midnight, followed by a long drive to the market, unloading boxes and a long drive home can be exhausting if done regularly. These are the markets that can handle large quantities of produce because of their sheer size, but all that has been said before about continuity of supply and quality still of vital importance.

One other factor that now shows real importance, much more so than in the previous categories, is that of packaging. Don't skimp on packaging. A visit to any of the regional markets will soon show the value of good packaging. By this means you are trying to project an image to the final customer.

A good quality box is a must. Not only does it look good, it will also protect your produce during the rigors of transport. Just stop to think for a minute how well *you* would have to be packed to be loaded onto a truck, driven over bumpy roads, unloaded and put into store, banged about, reloaded onto another truck, driven miles, unloaded, etc., when your only protection is a cardboard box! Remember the fresh produce is a lot more delicate and susceptible to damage than you are, so don't skimp. Also, remember to pack produce into appropriate boxes. No English produce should go into Dutch tomato trays, and banana boxes are for bananas, not lettuce or carrots.

The one problem with good quality packaging is the price. If you are only producing relatively small quantities of a range of products it may not be possible to develop your own packaging and logo to the upper standards. You are then limited to the materials you can purchase from your local supplier. Another option open to you may be to group together for marketing purposes with other local growers to enable you to gain the benefits of bulk purchase and possible transportation and other benefits.

National Marketing Agents

These organizations are basically large commercial companies that obtain produce from both their own production units and from a range of other growers. The arrangements vary from a service similar to the local wholesaler to contracts for product. All of these may enable to you to reach outlets otherwise beyond the reach of the smaller grower, namely the major U.S. supermarkets. Ocean Spray was established as such a group for the cranberry growers. The mission of the organization was to open new markets. Of course, the innovation of the members and the people Ocean Spray employed has reached far beyond the original mission to the point of creating new products, thus providing new markets for members and other growers.

The supply of produce to these prestigious outlets can be fraught with difficulties but the rewards can be good. The standards laid down for supplies of product may be higher than those normally required by the regulatory groups, the times of deliveries can be very narrow and the quantities required may be large but the returns can be good, or at least more consistent than market prices. This latter point is often argued, but it can be proven time and time again that, taken over a season, the supermarkets return the best prices per unit of produce.

These prices can be bettered by the smaller grower if he or she specializes in out-of-season production, in which case the wholesale markets will almost certainly return the best prices. This premise points to another major consideration for the smaller grower—that of specialization in either crops or timing of crops. One small word of caution with regard to specialization: Be sure there is a real market for your specialized crop.

If after all this you would still like to market to the national supermarkets there may be another way, via one of the national marketing cooperatives. Once again, volume and geographic location may prohibit joining one of these organizations as a member. It still may be possible to join a local marketing cooperative.

Cooperatives

These can offer many advantages to the smaller grower. By working together with similar-minded growers marketing costs can be reduced, particularly transportation and packaging costs. The provision of a centralized packhouse can enable specialized grading and processing equipment to be purchased since the cost is spread out over a number of growers. This in turn gives a better quality product to enable the cooperative members to compete with the larger suppliers on more equal terms.

Cooperation can then lead to other advantages for the smaller grower. These can include the passing on of discounts for bulk purchases of other requisites such as fertilizers, chemicals, etc. Even machinery pools can be formed to allow the purchase and use of specialized machinery. The machinery may not need to be that specialized to be advantageous. A polyethylene-laying machine may be above the reach of an individual grower but if several growers or the cooperative purchase it, the cost is spread and the growers can benefit from the use of such equipment.

If there is no cooperative in your local area that you can join, it may be possible to form one. Grants may be available and there are several organizations that help people set up cooperatives, both from marketing and other production standpoints.

What are the disadvantages? The main one appears to be the regulations that have to be provided when a number of people own and run (via a board of directors) the company (cooperative). These are set to ensure the fair use of the company and the equal treatment of all members. At times cooperatives seem to suppress individuality, but most cooperatives work well for the mutual benefit of all members. Each member of a cooperative has a real say in how the organization is run, unlike some of the other organizations already mentioned. This may suit some people and not others. In the end the final choice is yours and should be the form of marketing most apt to your own situation.

PACKAGING AND PRESENTATION

Packaging and presentation of any product in any marketplace is important. Vendors using sound, tested market procedures will yield the quickest sales and maximum profits. Produce attractively packaged and reasonably priced will result in great buyer interest.

Selecting Produce

For maximum freshness, gather the produce immediately before marketing the product. For example, if the vegetable or fruit is susceptible to wilting from prolonged exposure (such as carrots, leafy greens, broccoli, etc.), pick or dig the crop just before transporting to market or opening to the public. If time necessitates gathering the crop earlier, store it in a cool, protected place to ensure maximum freshness.

Your success in the marketplace—whether at the farmers market, roadside stand or delivery to middlemen—will greatly increase if your harvest and display produce are at the proper stage of development and the presentation is professional. Buyers traditionally pass by dirty root crops and insect- or disease-damaged produce in favor of clean, edible fruits and vegetables. Mechanical damage will also detract from the overall appeal of the produce.

If pesticides or other chemical additives were used in the production of your crop, be sure to read the pesticide label to ensure proper usage and harvest intervals. Specific guidelines for harvesting and chemical use are available from your local cooperative extension office.

Customers want to believe that they are getting wholesome foods, fresh from the garden.

Packaging

The vast majority of buyers purchasing at a farmers market, farm shop, roadside stand or even a pick-your-own plot are interested in a quantity for immediate use. Therefore, it is important to make this smaller, convenient-sized package available for that demand.

A few purchasers at these markets and larger volume purchasers, such as caterers, middlemen, etc., are more interested in volume packaging. Tailor your packaging to your market, just as you do your product line.

For example, carrots and beets can be tied in bunches—tops intact; tomatoes, peppers and green beans can be packaged in small containers or plastic bags; small fruits such as cherries, strawberries or raspberries can be placed in small plastic boxes or bags; potatoes and onions can be packaged in plastic bags. Select a container that will make the most of what your produce has to offer the consumer.

Remember, when selecting your packaging, don't confuse your customers with mixed messages. If the produce is "certified organically grown" with an environmentally safe emphasis, it would be unwise to use plastics in your packaging.

Displaying Your Produce

Remember, no matter how you are marketing your produce, the way you display the produce serves as your advertisement. Well-planned, attractive displays not only put the produce in the best light but show your commitment to quality as a producer.

Arrange bulk and prepackaged produce to permit buyer selection without excessive handling that may result in damage to the remainder of the produce. In the past, producers have displayed taste samples to show the quality of the produce. This has been a standing tradition in farmers markets, roadside stands and farm shops. Innovative marketers have utilized this same technique with other buyers as well.

Pricing

Consumers expect fresh, high-quality produce at prices that are lower than or competitive with other retail outlets when they shop for produce directly. Produce may be priced by the piece, count, package or container and weight. If a vendor plans to sell by weight, state law requires that the scale must carry an official and current inspection seal.

Remember, potential customers are often reluctant to ask prices. List your prices—each price, bag, crate, etc.—on an easily read sign in a conspicuous place. Hint: Add your name, address and telephone number for further buyer contact.

Word of mouth from satisfied buyers can work to your best advantage for future sales.

KNOW THE LAWS AND REGULATIONS

Sales Tax

Depending on how you market your produce, you may be faced with collecting sales tax. Direct marketers will need a sales tax license, if required in your area. The department of revenue for each state will assist you in complying with all laws. For information on applicable sales tax at the state, county and city levels, contact the appropriate departments of revenue.

Health Ordinances

State and county health laws for direct produce marketers vary throughout the country. Contact your county and state health departments to clarify requirements.

Liability Laws

Inform your insurance agent in writing of your business practices. Landowners involved in a pick-your-own operation must resolve any potentially hazardous conditions. Remember, you are liable for accidents on your property. It is better to be safe than sorry.

In addition, remember that as a grower you are responsible for your product. Know the health laws and limits to liability that could have an impact on your business operation.

Chemical Use

Make sure that all chemicals used are licensed, and that you monitor the use and approximate intervals between use and harvest. For information on approved chemicals, contact your state department of agriculture, plants division.

Summary

To summarize then, the points to remember are as follows:

- Grow for a specific market—one that suits your requirements.
- Only grow for those markets you can conveniently reach, or select another site.
- Spread your market outlets as much as possible so you do not rely on a single outlet. If your local retailer goes bust or unexpectedly stops trading, can you cope? To use the age-old expression, "Don't put all your eggs in one basket."
- Consider how you present your produce. Packaging and presentation are also market tools.
- Make sure you comply with all regulations impacting your production and marketing.
- Consider all the options before making any decisions.

All the points raised in this chapter are equally relevant whether the produce is chemically or organically produced.

CHAPTER 3

How to Grow:
Soils and Their Management

 *H*aving looked at the varieties of marketing options in the previous chapter we now come back down to earth—literally. It is now time to consider the major resource of your holding other than the human factor, and that is the soil. The maintenance of a fertile soil should be the prime consideration of anyone lucky enough to be a custodian of land, whether they are owner or tenant. This major resource, on which many nations' prosperity has been built, has a vast influence on your own profitability. It is a fragile ecosystem of its own that can be easily damaged, but can be improved and at times vastly improved. It needs to be carefully understood and treated with respect.

A good soil makes life easier, a poor soil makes the struggle much harder; but take heart, those of you who have a poor soil—you can improve it. However, there is no quick route, just good husbandry and understanding of this most basic of resources. "The answer lies in the soil" is an old adage but there was never a truer one. The answer to many growing problems lies in a good healthy plant, and that needs a good, fertile, well-nurtured soil. So how do we achieve this ideal soil?

The obvious answer to this question is to ensure you buy or rent good soil with an advantageous aspect in the first place. These should be the prime considerations; but, thinking back to the previous chapter, it is no good finding the ideal site—a good, fertile soil with southern exposure—if there is no outlet for the resulting mountain of produce. So when making an initial choice, find the best site within a reasonable distance of your target market. It is unlikely that we will find the "ideal" soil, so it is better to see what the soil is, look at its structure and see what can be done to improve it.

What is soil? According to *The Concise Oxford Dictionary* soil is

an "upper layer of earth in which plants grow, consisting of disinte-
grated rock usually with an admixture of organic remains, mold." For
all practical purposes, soil is a medium into which plant roots forage
searching for the nutrients to sustain the growth of the plant. It also
enables the plant to support itself to gain maximum benefit from the
available light. So the soil needs to be compact enough to support the
plant, yet porous enough to allow the roots to forage easily to obtain
the foods the plant requires. It is a hard compromise to achieve, and the
level of difficulty depends on the properties of the main constituents
of your soil. These are sand, silt and clay. A fourth constituent that can
have a major effect on the soil structure is organic matter. It is the
varying properties of sand, silt and clay that determine the classification of the soil (Figure 3.1).

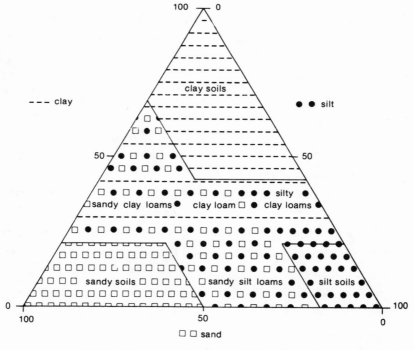

Figure 3.1. Soil classification. Soils can be classified by estimating the percentage at each fraction on the diagram.

SOIL ANALYSIS

One way of determining your soil structure is to fill a jam jar or other suitable glass container halfway with soil, add water until it is about three-quarters full, add some vinegar, put a lid on and give it a good shake. Shake for about one minute and then put it down immediately. The vinegar helps to settle the fine clay particles quickly. The various fractions of sand, silt and clay will separate and

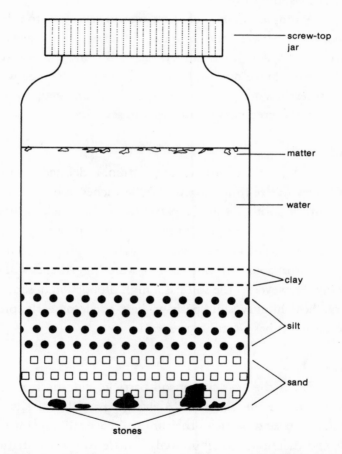

Figure 3.2. Separation of sand, silt and clay in jam jar. Approximate proportions of 50% silt, 40% sand and 10% clay give a sandy silt loam.

an approximate proportion of each can be ascertained. (See Figure 3.2.)

The sand and stones will be at the bottom, followed by the silt, with the clay on top. Any organic matter will be either floating on the surface or on top of the clay. From this you can check quickly on the soil type of your holding. Remember, though, the soil types can vary considerably in a small area, and there may be considerable variations across your land, especially if it is on a slope. This can influence decisions on where to site various parts of the holding, such as greenhouses, buildings, etc.

A simpler method of assessing soil texture is to rub a sample of moist soil between the thumb and fingers. A sandy soil will feel gritty, a silt soil will feel smooth and silky and a clay soil will feel sticky. Why do we need to know these properties? The workability and base fertility of the soil depend on this basic makeup, and if we look at the main ingredients in turn we can see why.

Sand

Sand, by international convention, is defined as soil particles which vary in size from 0.08 to 0.0008 inches in diameter. They are made up of solid, insoluble particles of base rock, which greatly improve the aeration and drainage of the soil but provide no real nutrients for the plant. A soil with a reasonable proportion of sand will be easily workable, will not become waterlogged and will warm up quickly. However, if the soil has a high proportion of sand it will be a dry, hot, hungry soil, perhaps best used for early production, especially if it has a southern exposure.

Silt

Silt is the next size of soil particle, ranging from 0.0008 to 0.00008 inches in diameter. Although particles of silt are much smaller than sand particles they are still basically unweathered minerals and therefore contribute only a little to plant nutrition. Their presence will increase the water holding capacity, but they can impede drainage by blocking up pore spaces. They will give the soil more bite.

Clay

Clay particles are the smallest, being less than 0.00008 inches in diameter, and are very different from sand and silt particles. They are the products of chemical weathering of other soil constituents. These particles are extremely small and are in fact of colloidal size because of this they have a large surface area in relation to their mass. This means they have many surface atoms and, if they are electrically charged, they can attract ions from the soil solution and hold them on their surface. Usually they are negatively charged and attract the positively charged ions or cations, for example, potassium, calcium, etc. Therefore they are the major influence on the fertility of the soil.

It can be seen that the fertility of a soil is in direct relationship to the proportion of clay particles within the soil, all other aspects being equal. This is fine, but from the grower's point of view the workability of the soil has an inverse relationship to the amount of clay; that is, the greater the proportion of clay the heavier the soil and, therefore, the more difficult to work it becomes. Once again, the best soils are in the middle range, providing an ease of workability yet having a sufficiently large proportion of clay to be fertile and provide a buffer reservoir of nutrients for optimum plant growth. While this area is not covered in great depth, it should enable readers to understand the potential of various soil types.

We have now looked at the basic makeup of the soil; now we must consider it in more depth—literally—and look at the soil profile.

SOIL PROFILE

The soil profile can have a profound effect on any individual soil type. It is not just the top nine inches of soil with which we must be concerned but also what is underneath. A soil profile is a vertical section through the soil and to gain a full insight needs to extend at least three feet down, and preferably more, to see what is below. For this purpose the soil profile is divided into distinct layers or horizons that may or may not be easily recognized. There are usually considered

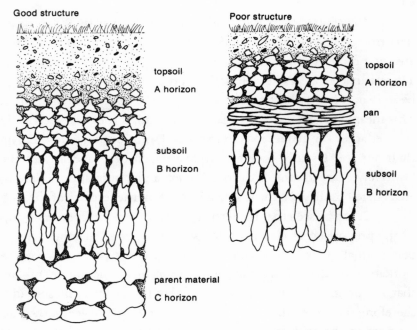

Figure 3.3. Soil profiles, showing good and poor structure, horizons and a pan.

to be three horizons: the A horizon, or topsoil; the B horizon, or subsoil; and the C horizon, or parent material.

The depths of these individual horizons can vary considerably. The A horizon, or topsoil, can vary from just a few inches to several feet but is normally nine to twelve inches as this is the normal depth of cultivation.

When assessing a site, the subsoil or B horizon can be of great importance. It may be a heavy clay that will impede drainage and could have an adverse effect on the topsoil, or it could be a free-draining subsoil overlaid by a clay topsoil. Many combinations can be found; being aware of what you have and how this influences cultivations and plant growth can make your life much easier. This may prevent problems occurring or help provide reasons why certain things have been happening.

An impervious clay layer or a hard "pan" in the subsoil will restrict drainage and plant root growth and hence reduce the cropping potential of the land. It may be possible to help the situation by careful management or the use of mechanical equipment such as subsoilers to reduce these problems.

As we have seen, soil texture and soil profile can have a great influence on the cropping potential of an individual site. Those areas that have a good soil are usually the most expensive to buy, with good reason. It is difficult to change the soil texture appreciably. It can be done but will be a long-term project, the full fruits of which may not be seen in the lifetime of those starting the process. Having said that, it is no reason not to plan into the management of the holding all the techniques that will help to achieve this. At the very least, this will prevent a deterioration of this most basic of the grower's or mankind's resources. This form of conservation or improvement is actively encouraged by the current organic movement as a vital part of any growing or farming system.

Remember that soil texture is, if you like, the mix of the basic ingredients of the soil in their physical proportions. Obviously, to change this physical proportion vast amounts of sand or clay would need to be added. Take heart though, especially those of you who have a heavy soil; there is one area we can change relatively easily, and that is soil structure.

SOIL STRUCTURE

The analogy of a house may help to explain soil structure. If we assume the wood, bricks and mortar to be sand, silt and clay (soil texture), they can be put together in the same proportions as to construct a house, but the actual style of the house can vary considerably using the same amounts of wood, brick and mortar. The same is true with soil, and this arrangement of the soil particles is known as its structure.

A good soil structure will allow water to enter the soil easily

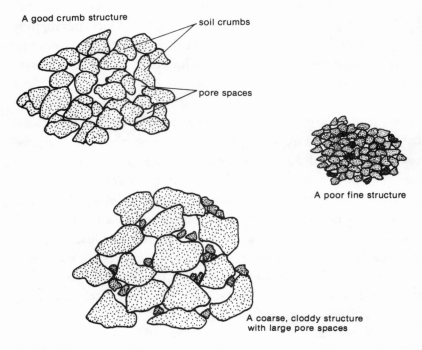

Figure 3.4. Soil crumb structure.

and excess moisture to drain freely from it. It also allows air to permeate the soil, since plant roots cannot live without air. With a good crumb structure cultivations and the preparation of a good tilth will be easy, and the soil is less likely to be damaged.

What do we need to obtain a good crumb structure? Ideally the soil crumbs should be in the size range of 0.02 to 0.2 inches. The soil's ability to form a good crumb structure depends on the amounts of two constituents: clay and humus (organic matter). I have already mentioned that clay particles help to bind the soil with larger particles, but if the proportion of clay is too high the soil will be impervious. Humus or organic matter will also have the same effect in binding the particles together to form crumbs. It is here that we have the greatest opportunity to improve the soil.

We all know that we should add compost or other organic

matter to a soil, but we do not necessarily know why. It will improve a sandy soil by helping to bind the particles to stabilize the soil and make it more water retentive; with a clay soil it helps to separate the clay particles into crumbs and make the soil more porous. The addition of organic matter will help the structure of the soil immensely. It will also give other benefits that we will discuss a little later.

A good soil structure will provide the best conditions for plant growth. To be really effective it needs to continue as far as possible down the soil profile, and ideally throughout the subsoil or B horizon. It obviously becomes more difficult to modify the soil structure the further down the profile one goes, but steps that can be taken to do this are covered in the following section, "Soil Management." Before moving on to soil management, let's briefly summarize soil structure.

Soil texture identifies the proportions of the major building blocks of the soil, that is, sand, silt and clay, within the soil profile. The soil structure is the way these particles are actually arranged. It is this latter that we can influence most, and to provide good crop growth a good structure is essential. It is the soil structure that we, as custodians of the land, can most easily improve or destroy depending on how we manage our soil.

SOIL MANAGEMENT

The most important aspect of soil management is timing of the various operations. Anyone who has worked the soil for pleasure will know the difference of working a soil at the correct time, especially on a clay soil. If the clay soil is too wet it can be sticky, while a few drying days later it is like concrete and nothing can break up the lumps. It is bad enough trying to time it correctly on a small vegetable patch, but when the pressures of running a commercial holding are applied to the situation, it can be very difficult to say, "It's a bit wet today—I'll leave the rototilling until the soil is a bit drier."

Waiting until tomorrow may be fine if time permits, but if the plants have been ready for planting for a week and there is a bad

Rototilling light sandy soil in good condition is a delight for any market gardener.

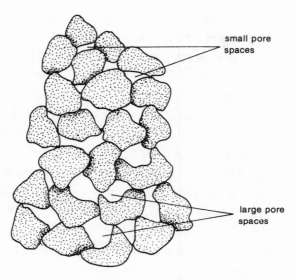

Figure 3.5. Soil pores. The small pores hold water, the large pores, air. They are compressed by compaction.

weather forecast, what alternative does a grower have, except to do the job at a less than ideal time? This incorrect timing of cultivation can at least provide the plant or seed with inferior conditions and at worst drastically damage the soil structure. It is hoped that any damage to the the soil structure will be limited, but it can be virtually permanent. For example, lasting damage was done to many fields in East Anglia, England, where sugar beet was harvested in wet conditions in autumn 1987. In many cases, the damage to fields incurred at the access points is irreparable.

Damage to the soil can be done in two ways. First of all, the smearing action of a lot of cultivation equipment, especially plows and rotary cultivators, can cause major problems of panning, especially if cultivation is always done at a constant depth. Certain soils are more susceptible to cultivation pans than others, especially those with a high clay content. Pans are created by the smearing action of the machinery, which makes the soil below impervious and so impedes drainage and the passage of air, both so important in the root zone.

They can be prevented by varying the depth of cultivations, ensuring the soil is in a suitable condition for cultivation and using subsoilers. To gain maximum benefit from subsoiling, this operation needs to be done when the lower levels of the soil are relatively dry. This ensures much greater fracturing as the blade of the machine is pulled through the soil. There is also a second advantage of timing this operation to coincide with a drier soil. As the leg of a subsoiler extends some two to three feet down, it requires a fair amount of power from any tractor pulling it. This tractor will do less damage to the soil in drier conditions. There is no point in using a subsoiler to alleviate the problem of a pan in a soil yet to increase compaction and smearing action in the topsoil by doing so.

The second way in which soil structure can be damaged is by compaction of the soil. A good soil with a balance of the main ingredients of sand, silt, clay and organic matter will have a much better resistance to compaction than either a clay soil or a sandy soil, or in fact any soil lacking in organic matter. This is due to the ratio of pore spaces within the soil. The passage of machinery over the soil will have the effect of closing up the large pore spaces. The weight of the equipment pressing downward pushes the individual soil particles closer together. This reduces the amount of pore space and, hence, the speed with which water can be both absorbed into the soil and drained away. It will obviously affect the amount of air in the soil as well. Both those factors can in turn limit the growth potential of any crop in such a soil. The repeated use of a Rototiller on clay soils, continued with a lack of regular dressings of organic matter, will also destroy the structure of the soil, even with correct timing of operations.

We have now seen that working the soil can cause real damage to the structure and fertility of the soil. What can we as growers do to ensure that damage is minimized and the structure maintained or improved?

First, the easiest way any tiller of the soil can ensure that he or she does minimal damage is by timing all operations to coincide with the correct soil moisture content. A sandy soil can be broken down to

A pedestrian Rototiller with a rake attachment for seedbed preparation is a relatively inexpensive and effective piece of equipment, especially for the beginning market gardener.

a fine tilth when dry, but with a clay soil timing is critical; too dry and the lumps are too hard, too wet and it's like modelling clay, and the cultivations will do further damage to the structure.

Second, the depth and type of cultivation equipment used should be varied, if indeed any form of cultivation is used. The specific machine should be matched to soil type and moisture content to get optimum results. Next, use equipment that has a low ground pressure and make as few passes as possible. It has been estimated that in normal spring cultivations and sowing approximately ninety percent of the soil surface is covered by wheelings at one time or another. To put it another way, the potential for compaction is ninety percent of the field! This may lead to the conclusion that it would be best for organic and commercial farmers to use a no-cultivation system, but this would only be so if no equipment or wheels pass over the land.

The third way we can maintain and even improve soil structure is by the addition of organic matter. This will have many effects: It will improve structure, increase water holding capacity and nutrient supply (especially nitrogen) and make the soil more resistant to compaction. Such improvements will make the soil much easier to manage, and the timing of cultivations will be less crucial.

There is a variety of ways in which organic matter can be added to a soil. Sufficient organic matter will exist in pasture land soil which is newly plowed. It has long been known that the soil is vastly better when a permanent pasture is cultivated. This effect only lasts for a few seasons, and further organic matter must be incorporated with subsequent cultivations. On natural soils the residual plant material from the native vegetation dies and returns to the soil, and a slow increase in organic matter occurs in the topsoil. In an intensively cropped system, the waste plant material is often removed from the field. This may be done to help prevent a buildup of pest and disease organisms on the site. On a market garden no resources should be wasted, so any surplus plant material should be returned to the soil to help maintain its structure and fertility. To prevent the spread of pests and disease organisms, the material should be composted.

Using hay as a compost element is often ideal for organic market gardeners.

When considering the long-term effects on soil of intensive cropping, remember that a large proportion of the plant material grown on the site will not be returned to the soil site because it is the marketable product. This needs to be replaced in some other form. Farmyard manure is the most common form of organic matter to be added to the soils. This can be added directly or composted with the holding waste and then spread on the land. But it should be remembered that farmyard manure is a variable product and the amount of nutrients it will supply to a soil can vary.

Straw is another organic material that may be readily available in certain parts of the country. Some words of caution are needed, though, if fresh straw is added to a soil. Because of its low protein content (proteins are required by soil bacteria to break down the material), it will actually reduce nitrogen levels for the succeeding crop. The addition of 4.5 tons of straw per acre will lock up 62.5 pounds of nitrogen per acre from that available for a crop.

Another useful way of adding organic matter to soils is by green manuring. This is the practice of growing a "crop" and incorporating all of it directly into the topsoil. It will be no stranger to devotees of organic growing. In many areas it can aid soil conservation and soil improvement.

One major factor that has led to the problems of soil erosion in some areas is that of leaving a soil uncovered over winter. This can lead to topsoil being washed off sloping land by winter rains. The use of green manures will stabilize the soil during this time and give it additional organic matter when incorporated in spring. In fact, green manures can be beneficial at any time when a soil is not to be cropped for a while. Not only will they stabilize the soil, they can help retain moisture and suppress weeds, and, depending on the plants used, help to draw up nutrients from the subsoil as well. This latter will occur especially if deep-rooted types such as lucerne are used.

A good rotation of crops also plays an important part in maintaining soil fertility. As crops have differing needs, the soil is given a chance to recover, which is not the case in a monocrop situation. Where possible, some form of rotation should be used. Having said that, it could be that specialization in cropping can be necessary to ensure the economic success of a modern market garden. If this is so, a real effort should be made to prevent the possible harmful effects of monocropping. The use of farmyard manure, compost or green manures will help restore a more natural balance.

REASONS FOR CULTIVATION

We have examined the importance of timing cultivation with regard to the possible damage to soils. In many respects, if we reflect on the previous section, a noncultivation system may seem appropriate—so why do we cultivate the soil? The basic answer to this question is to provide suitable conditions for root development for the plant.

We have seen how compaction and naturally formed "pans" can hinder root development, impede drainage and generally make life difficult for the plant. Therefore, the aim of any cultivation must be to improve conditions for the plant. It will also aid the incorporation of organic matter and fertilizers. There is now a vast range of cultivation equipment available to help the modern market gardener. Great care must be exercised when choosing equipment. Will it do the job I want? Is it the best type of machine for my growing system, my soil type and my budget? Cultivation equipment will be discussed in Chapter 6.

CHAPTER 4

Crop Requirements and Nutrition

*I*n the previous chapter we examined the soil and recommended ways to provide optimum conditions for the crop roots to develop. We now need to consider the nutritional requirements of crops.

A crop will only reach its full potential for a grower if it is supplied with the right amounts of the basic nutrients required. This will, of course, vary from crop to crop, but before anyone goes out and spreads liberal amounts of fertilizers to promote growth, we should ascertain what is required and how much. So where do we start?

Chemical fertilizers are expensive and not permitted if you are an organic grower, so it is always a good idea to have your soil analyzed for its nutritional status. This can be done at a cost by various laboratories, or it can be arranged through your local cooperative extension service office, or even by fertilizer manufacturers. Kits can be bought for do-it-yourself analysis, but these will not be as accurate. They will, however, give a good indication of nutritional status and should register any changes in this status.

Of the three main plant foods—nitrogen, phosphorus and potassium—nitrogen cannot easily be analyzed and has to be estimated from past cropping.

NITROGEN (N)

Nitrogen is probably the most important plant food. This is because it is very difficult to determine the optimum amount to provide for a crop. If there is too little the crop won't grow; too much, and maturity may be delayed and the fertilizer is wasted or results in environmental damage. The soil's natural reserve of nitrogen is contained in the organic matter within the soil. In mineral soils the vast majority of organic matter is in the topsoil, so that is where the naturally available nitrogen will be found.

This organic matter is continuously being broken down by soil bacteria and converted to a form which plants can readily absorb. This process has two stages: proteins in the organic matter are first converted to ammonia, which is then converted to nitrates by the nitrifying bacteria in the soil for the plants to take up. This all occurs happily when oxygen or air is present. If the soil becomes waterlogged and no oxygen is present, another range of bacteria attacks the nitrates and releases nitrogen gas.

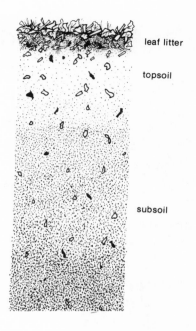

leaf litter

topsoil

subsoil

Figure 4.1. Distribution of organic matter in the soil profile, with normally about five percent organic matter in topsoil, decreasing with depth.

The importance of having a well-drained soil with a good structure can be seen once again. We can apply artificial fertilizers to make up the difference between the crop's requirements and the amount of nitrogen naturally available in the soil. The big question is how much to apply. As nitrates are readily soluble, the timing and amounts applied are critical if any excess is not to be leached out into drainage water before the plants can absorb it.

As nitrates are so highly soluble and easily move through the soil in the soil water, it is difficult to assess the nitrogen levels in the soil accurately. The normal system used relates to the organic matter

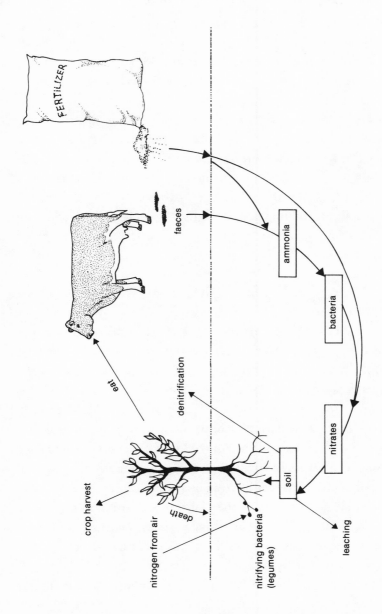

Figure 4.2. The nitrogen cycle. Under natural conditions plant nutrients are recycled. When a crop is harvested and removed this can lead to a lowering of nitrogen and organic matter levels.

content of the soil and, therefore, relates directly to previous cropping of the land in question. An arable growing system with no pasture included in the rotation will produce an organic matter content of one to three percent, as opposed to that of a plowed-up ley where levels of organic matter may reach five to ten percent.

As we have seen, nitrogen levels relate directly to organic matter levels; hence, an intensive arable system will produce only a little natural nitrogen and will require more artificial fertilizer. The organic content of the soil should be increased by incorporating bulky organics such as farmyard manure or compost, using a rotation including leys and applying green manures, especially those utilizing leguminous plants such as lupins or clovers which fix gaseous nitrogen in their root nodules.

PHOSPHORUS (P)

Phosphorus is vital to the plant for respiration and in the actively growing parts such as roots and shoots. It is also required in the seed for germination. Unlike nitrogen it is not leached from the soil. This is because the inorganic phosphorous becomes insoluble in the soil and accumulates from repeated fertilizer dressings. Therefore, phosphate deficiency is relatively uncommon, especially in the heavier clay soils of the Midwest and the South. Light soils and the acid soils of New England are more likely to require regular dressings as the phosphates are rapidly converted to an unavailable form. Yet, once the phosphate has been absorbed by the plant, it remains mobile and can be moved from older parts to the actively growing areas.

As crops such as potatoes, brassicas and roots have a higher demand for phosphates, it may be possible to rotate the application of phosphate so it is applied only before a high-demand crop. It should also be noted that to obtain maximum yields one has to apply more phosphate than the crop will actually take up. It should be placed near the roots of the crop due to its immobility in the soil; the roots have to forage for it, so a good soil structure will help this process.

Brassicas have a high demand for phosphate.

Compacted or waterlogged soils will deny plants phosphates. If artificial media (loamless composts) are used for plant raising, ensure that sufficient phosphate is added as there will be no natural reserves in the compost. Phosphate can be leached out of soilless composts, so the use of slow-release forms is recommended.

Bonemeal is the traditional fertilizer but this is now believed to be unsuitable; natural rock phosphates or super or triple super-phosphates should be used.

POTASSIUM (K OR POTASH)

Potash is generally considered to be the food for flowers and fruit. It is also used in the plant as an osmotic regulator and helps to keep it healthy. It also plays a part in the control of photosynthesis and respiration. When in the correct balance with nitrogen, it will increase the plant's resistance to chill damage, drought and disease. These

Tomatoes may require heavy dressings of potash, but in balance with other nutrients.

latter points can be of great value of the grower. The ideal balance to achieve is a one-to-one ratio of nitrogen to potassium within the plant. Plants are capable of taking up more potassium than they actually need (luxury levels), however, and this can have an effect on soil reserves, particularly where leafy crops are harvested young. For this to occur, high levels of nitrogen need to be applied.

The balance of potash with another plant food, magnesium, is also important, especially in crops such as tomatoes. Applying heavy dressings of potash can upset this balance and lead to a deficiency of magnesium. For this reason, when applying heavy dressing, such as for cherry tomatoes, part of the application should be made as magnesium sulfate (kieserite) to maintain the balance in its correct ratio of nine-to-one potassium to magnesium. Potassium is readily recycled from organic matter and is present in large amounts in young soil, but due to its solubility may be leached from old soils. It is also easily leached from soilless composts and sandy soils with a low organic matter content. In horticulture, the most commonly used fertilizers are potassium sulfate (sulfate of potash) and potassium nitrate. The latter also supplies nitrogen and is commonly used in liquid feeds; it is hygroscopic (absorbs moisture from the air) and needs to be kept dry.

MAGNESIUM (MG)

Magnesium deficiency is probably one of the most common deficiencies to occur in intensive horticulture. It is most likely to exist in light soils with a low organic matter content or where heavy dressings of potash have been applied (see "Potassium"). Magnesium deficiency can also be a problem in lime-rich soils. To counteract it, the most common fertilizers used are magnesian lime, which raises the pH as well as adding magnesium (for pH see "Calcium") or kieserite (magnesium sulfate). If a deficiency occurs in a growing crop, spraying with magnesium sulfate (the pure form of which is Epsom salts) will have an immediate effect.

CALCIUM (CA OR LIME)

Calcium needs to be considered in two ways, first as plant food where a deficiency shows in a variety of symptoms (Table 4.1). The second way calcium needs to be understood is in its most commonly applied form—lime. In the past lime was also considered to be vital to "keep the soil sweet." As with most old sayings, this bears more than a grain of truth. Lime is the major soil conditioner. It is used to correct the pH of the soil as well as to supply calcium as a plant food. Generally speaking, if the pH is correct, in all likelihood there is enough calcium available as a food. So what is pH?

The pH scale is a measurement of the acidity or alkalinity of a soil. It is, in fact, a measurement of the hydrogen ion concentration in the soil. To enable this to be expressed in simple terms, a negative logarithmic scale is used. This gives a scale from 1 to 14—1 being acid, 14 alkaline and 7 the neutral point. In practice, the pH of soils generally lies between pH4 and pH8.5. Soil pH can be tested using either a BDH test kit or a pH meter. A pH test normally forms part of any soil analysis you may have done. It is worthwhile to have a pH test done regularly to ensure the ideal pH is being maintained for the crops grown. The chemically neutral point (pH7) is not necessarily ideal for all crops and it is more usual to aim for a pH of 6.5 in most soils.

A soil with a low pH, that is, acid, can easily have its pH raised nearer to a neutral level by the addition of lime. Before applying lime, two important points need to be remembered. First, as the pH scale is logarithmic, a pH of 5 is one hundred times more acid than a pH of 6 which is in turn ten times more acid than a pH of 7. Putting this another way, a pH of 5 is one hundred times more acid than a pH of 7. This will have an effect on the amount of lime required to raise the pH to optimal levels. The second important point to remember when applying lime is that it works slowly in the soil, so its full effect of neutralizing an acid soil is not complete for at least three years. If this point is not remembered, it is easy to overlime a soil. The potential of overliming or raising the pH too high is important as it is much easier to raise a soil's pH than reduce it.

Lime also has a secondary effect on soils. It can actually help to improve soil structure, particularly in clay soils. One word of caution though: Many clay soils have a relatively high pH, so check before using lime as a soil conditioner.

The main agents that act to reduce a soil's pH are acid rain (most of our rain is now polluted to a greater or lesser degree, but see "Sulphur"), farmyard manure and nitrogen fertilizers. Continuous cropping will also help to acidify a soil by plants removing calcium from the soil. The normally recommended agent to use to actively reduce a pH is sulphur (flowers of sulphur), which is expensive and difficult to apply.

The pH of a soil also has an effect on the availability of nutrients in the soil. Too high a pH can "lock up" certain nutrients, making them unavailable to the plant, and resulting in problems such as lime-induced chlorosis or iron deficiency. Commonly, too low a pH can have a similar effect (Table 4.2).

Crops also vary in their tolerance of pH. Most gardeners know rhododendrons like an acid soil and most brassicas like lime. A range of crops and their pH tolerances are given in Table 4.2.

Table 4.1. pH Tolerances of Crops

	Crop	pH (All figures approximate)
Vegetables	Beans	6.0–7.5
	Brassicas	6.5–7.5
	Carrots	5.5–7.0
	Celery	6.3–7.0
	Courgettes	5.5–7.0
	Garlic	5.5–7.5
	Leeks	6.0–8.0
	Lettuces	6.0–7.0
	Peppers	5.8–7.0
	Parsnips	5.5–7.5
	Potatoes	4.5–6.0
	Swedes	5.5–7.0
	Tomatoes	5.5–7.5
Fruit	Apples	5.5–6.5
	Blackberries	5.0–6.0
	Black Currants	6.0–8.0
	Gooseberries	5.0–6.5
	Grapes	6.0–7.0
	Pears	6.0–7.5
	Raspberries	5.0–6.5
	Stawberries	5.3–7.5

See Appendix 1 for liming materials

SULPHUR (S OR SULFATES)

Sulphur is a vital ingredient in the synthesis of chlorophyll within the plant. The deficiency, therefore, shows as a paling of the young leaves of the plant. Sulphur is not readily transported around the plant due to its insolubility. It is normally taken up in the sulfate form and, in the past, has not normally been added to a specific fertilizer, but has been supplied either from the soil's natural reserves, from recycling plant remains (organic matter) or as a sulfate formulation of other fertilizers. A major source of sulphur has also been from polluted air where sulphur dioxide has dissolved in rain to form sulfuric acid, that is, acid rain. With the reduction in the use of sulfates in fertilizer formulation and the non-recycling of organic matter combined with the modern clean-air policy, deficiencies may become more commonplace. In fact, it is now starting to appear in certain parts of the country and has basically been put down to the clean-air policy!

TRACE ELEMENTS

We now come to the group of nutrients known as trace elements. This group of nutrients, though vital to the plant's growth and general health, is required in small quantities, usually measured in parts per million (PPM). For this reason they are sometimes called micronutrients. Deficiencies of all these nutrients, with the possible exception of zinc, occur within the various parts of the United States. The locations of these potential deficiencies depend on soil type and pH (Table 4.3).

Manganese (Mn)

Manganese deficiency usually occurs on soils with a high pH, particularly if the high pH is due to overliming. It is also more prevalent in soils with a high organic matter content. As the pH drops, manganese becomes progressively more available to the plant, even to the extent that it can become toxic. This is another good reason for

Table 4.2. Major Nutrient Deficiency

	Nitrogen	Phosphorus	Potassium	Magnesium	Calcium	Sulphur
Deficiency most likely to occur	Intensively cropped land and low organic matter	Heavy clays, light sands and acid soils	Intensively cropped land	Lime-rich soils and low organic matter. Associated with heavy dressing	Acid soils	Only now showing deficiency
Veinal Chlorosis						
Intervenial Chlorosis		*	*	*		*
Darkening of older leaves						
Pale juvenile leaves		*	*	*	*	
Necrotic area on leaves	*					*
Premature leaf fall		*				
Root growth reductions						

	Nitrogen	Phosphorus	Potassium	Magnesium	Calcium	Sulphur
Deficiency most likely to occur	Intensively cropped land and low organic matter	Heavy clays, light sands and acid soils	Intensively cropped land	Lime-rich soils and low organic matter. Associated with heavy dressing	Acid soils	Only now showing deficiency
Plant growth reduction	*	*				*
Affect crop yield	*	*	*	*	*	*
Bud dormancy prolonged	*	*				
Cure for deficiency	Nitrogen fertilizers solid or liquid feed, quick acting	Phosphate fertilizers in root zones fast start seedbed	Potash fertilizers e.g., sulphate of potash, quick acting	In soil magnesian lime or kieserite plant foliar spay of magnesium (Epsom salts)	Soil lime but check pH Apply calcium at 14-day intervals	Use of sulphate fertilizers, e.g., super phosphate potassium, sulphate, etc.
Susceptible crops	All, except possibly legumes	Carrot, lettuce, broad bean, sweet corn	Spinach, leek, lettuce, cauli-flower, radish	Tomato, cauli-flower, cabbage, marrow,	Celery, lettuce, brassicas	Cabbage, leek, swede

Table 4.3. Trace Element Deficiency Systems

Nutrient	Occurrence	Symptoms	Remedial Action	Susceptible Crops
Manganese	Peaty soils above pH 6.5 and calcerous soils with poor drainage. Tractor wheelings	Interveinal chlorosis on new leaves	Avoid over-liming; foliar spray of mangan-ese sulfate	Pea, French bean, onion
Iron	High pH and water-logged soils	Interveinal chlorosis. Young leaves may be bleached white	Iron chelates	Fruit, especially apples, sweet corn, brassicas
Copper	Peat soils, especially recently reclaimed peats and organic chalky soils	New leaves greyish green, chlorotic and wilting	Copper sulfate applied to soil	Carrot, lettuce, onion, brassicas, celery
Boron	Light alkaline soils in high rainfall areas	Cracking of stems and petioles, distension of leaves, "hollow stem" in brassicas	Borax to soil or solubor foliar spray	Brassicas, celery, beet, carrot, lettuce
Molybdenum	Rare except on acid soils below pH 5.5	"Whiptail" of cauli-flowers, i.e., new leaves only have midrib. Plants blind	Raise pH to 6.5 and/or sodium or ammonium molybdate	Cauliflower and other brassicas
Zinc	Not recorded in U.S.			

ensuring that the pH of your soil is correct. Any deficiency can be corrected by a foliar spray of manganese sulfate at a rate of one ounce per four gallons per 9.5 square yards.

Iron (Fe)

Iron deficiency usually occurs on lime-rich soils, hence its common name of "lime-induced chlorosis." It affects the young leaves first. The problem can be overcome by reducing applications of lime and phosphates and by applying iron chelates.

Copper (Cu)

Copper deficiency normally only occurs in light sandy soils or organic soils overlying chalk. Plants suffering from it tend to go very dark. It can also be a problem with livestock. Deficiency can be rectified by copper sulfate sprays.

Boron (Bo)

Boron deficiency is most likely to occur in alkaline soils, especially in dry season. Cauliflowers and Chinese cabbage seem particularly sensitive. The problem can be rectified by applications of borax.

Molybdenum (Mo)

This shows itself as "whip tail" in brassicas, particularly cauliflowers. It is most prevalent in acid soils, particularly if the pH is below 6. Liming will normally correct the deficiency by raising the pH, or sodium molybdate can be used.

Zinc (Zn)

A zinc deficiency is rare and only associated with a very high pH. Zinc can be applied inadvertently to soils, as can other heavy metals, via sewage sludge to a toxic level. This has actually occurred and fields so affected have been rendered unuseable—zinc toxicity cannot be removed from soil. So if you use sewage sludge, please check for heavy metal contamination before spreading it on the land.

Table 4.3 lists the nutrients, where the deficiency is most likely to occur, common symptoms and recommended remedial action.

FARMYARD MANURE

I have already talked much about the soil-improving qualities of farmyard manure. Being organic, it has an important role to play in nutrition as well. Its main constituents are straw and dung, and as these are of vegetable origin they will return a complete range of nutrients to the soil. There is one possible problem with any form of organic matter: Its nutrient content can vary considerably. It will vary with the ratio of straw to dung and whether it has been composted or kept. It even varies according to which animals produced the dung, for example, chicken manure is very "sharp" or hot, as it has a high proportion of ammonia. Thus, it is difficult to ascertain at what rates the various nutrients are being applied. It is common practice, though, to reduce fertilizer dressings if the land has had a reasonable dressing of farmyard manure.

With crops where an accurate balance of plant foods is necessary, it would be better to use only well composted or lower levels of farmyard manure to minimize the variation in nutrition levels. Having said that, the benefits of regular dressings of farmyard manure far outweigh the disadvantages.

One important point worth mentioning in regard to the use of farmyard manure is the possibility of contaminants. Be careful where you obtain your farmyard manure. It is possible that chemicals and drugs, that is, antiboidics, growth hormones, etc., may still be contained within the waste of the animals. So before you fill up the back of your truck with a load of manure from a local farm, ranch or feedlot, find out if there have been any problems resulting in treatment to the livestock recently. Commercially marketed manures should present no problem.

CHAPTER 5

Cropping Possibilities

*H*aving covered crop requirements in the last chapter, we now need to examine the crops themselves. Before plans are made to grow specific crops, they should be considered in the overall context of the marketing plan (see Chapter 2). If the grower has spent time formulating a method of marketing, this in turn will suggest broad areas of cropping possibilities. For example, if growing for a supermarket outlet there is no point in diversifying into a crop that may totally change the marketing system.

Growing crops and marketing are so interlinked that they cannot realistically be separated. Someone growing for his or her own retail outlet or farm shop will, of necessity, grow a much wider range of crops than might otherwise prove economic. If running a pick-your-own enterprise, only crops suitable for such marketing methods make sense.

In this section, each group of crops and their general requirements and marketing possibilities will be considered. For detailed information about individual crops, major seed houses can provide an endless source, as can a number of books and periodical publications (see this book's bibliography for a few possibilities).

VEGETABLES

This group covers a very wide range of individual crops. This range of crops can be grouped into three main classifications: brassicas, legumes and roots. This classification has many advantages. It is useful from the nutritional aspect, as crops within these groups will tend to have similar requirements. It is also useful from a pest and disease aspect as it allows rotation of cropped areas, which prevents a buildup

Brassica is easy to establish and is a popular vegetable among market gardeners.

of soil-borne problems. This classification can also aid in the management of the holding.

BRASSICAS

This group includes all types of cabbages, cauliflowers, sprouts, broccoli, swedes, turnips, radishes and kohlrabi. All these crops prefer an alkaline soil (it helps to prevent club root), and they need to be planted into firm soil to produce quality crops. Combined, these two requirements aid the management of the holding, enabling the grower to produce the conditions required by the crops on a larger area of land; hence production costs are reduced by efficient use of machinery, chemicals and fertilizers, etc.

If you are liming in order to maintain the correct pH (see Chapter 4), it makes sense to follow this operation by planting the crops that will gain maximum benefit from it, that is, brassicas.

Vegetables of this group like a firm soil—in fact, very few

plants like their roots in a settling soil—but growing most brassicas in a light fluffy soil will produce light fluffy sprouts and loose-headed cabbages. In the old days it was believed that a brassica was firmed enough at planting when it could not be pulled out of the ground with a sharp tug—the leaf ripped instead.

Freshly incorporated manure in the ground to be used for brassicas is also to be avoided as it can produce soft heads. This is due to an imbalance of nitrogen and potassium. Though the cabbage family is generally considered to be a gross feeder, the correct balance of nutrients must be maintained to produce good-quality crops. Potassium is especially important for cauliflowers.

The leafy brassicas and cauliflowers especially are very susceptible to any check in the growing regime, particularly after planting out. With care, the plant can be controlled if a modern plug seedling is used, but after transplanting any check can reduce the quality of the product.

It is possible to program harvesting brassicas over a prolonged season with the aid of many excellent modern varieties. Most brassicas that have been bred for the commercial grower are F1 hybrids. These have the advantage of evenness in cropping, that is, all from a similar sowing/transplanting date will mature over a few days. This can greatly aid mechanization and harvesting operations, and it can provide continuity in volume if your market requires that. It could be a disadvantage in a farm shop situation, as you may have a glut for a week and then no more. In this latter situation, the use of "open pollinated" varieties, which are more variable in harvest date, may be more appropriate.

Spacing of the plants is another important aspect. By varying the spacing a particular size of cabbage can be produced. Check what size head your market requires and match this to a variety and spacing that will produce this size. Many modern varieties can actually be grown closer than is at first thought normal due to advances in plant breeding, and the market generally seems to prefer a smaller product. By varying the spacing, it is possible to grow to your customers' requirements, be they retail, catering or supermarkets.

In summary, brassicas prefer a fertile, well-drained soil that is firm, and they benefit from additions of lime. Cauliflowers grow better on lighter land than cabbages and sprouts.

It is impossible to give accurate recommendations for fertilizer applications. For a general guide, a phosphate and potash application of 50 to 100 units is required, but cauliflowers may need 150 units of potash. Nitrogen requirements, as we saw in the previous chapter, depend on previous cropping but 150 to 200 units may be needed. Don't give any brassicas too much nitrogen, however; it will cause problems. It is best to split this dressing into two applications.

Herbicides can be used for weed control as can mechanical methods. Weeds are not usually a problem once the foliage touches from plant to plant, so the use of a stale seedbed will be useful in controlling weeds and ensuring firm soil.

As a group, brassicas offer a good marketing potential because it is possible to supply some form of them over a long period of time. If you are in an area where brassicas are grown in abundant quantities, they may not be best suited for a market garden crop except to supply a local market or retail outlet where the freshness of a local supply can be advantageous.

Pests and Diseases—Club root has already been mentioned as a problem. Good general hygiene, including sterilization of propagation areas and equipment, and care in the use of brought-in plants on the holding can all play an important part in ensuring this disease does not infect your land. It can be brought in on machinery and even on boots.

Other diseases that can cause problems on brassicas include alternaria leaf spot. This usually appears from July to September and initial infection seems to coincide with harvesting of oilseed rape in which alternaria can be endemic. At present, there are commercial products that provide effective chemicals for control.

The diseases ring spot and leaf spot (not to be confused with alternaria) can be problematic in wet weather beginning in August. Using wider spacing can help to control these two diseases.

Organic pest control has become very popular among market gardeners. Here Tagetes has been planted to dissuade aphids and other pests from attacking the brassicas.

Pseudomonas, a bacteria that causes black water-soaked lesions, can be seed-borne. It is spread by water splash and can get into a crop from an infected water supply. Good hygiene and efficient removal and burial of trash assist a great deal in preventing major problems as pools of infection cannot build up.

Pests of brassicas include the dreaded cabbage-root fly. This pest is attracted by smell to the brassica plant, be it crop or weed, and lays its eggs at the base. The hatching grubs then eat their way into the plant, causing damage and death. There are in fact three generations of cabbage-root fly. The first coincides with cow-parsley flowers—usually for a five-week period in May and June. Only young plants are susceptible, and modifications to the planting program can help to overcome this problem. The second generation emerges in July and August; and the third, which does not always occur, comes in September and is normally only a problem on sprouts.

Other pests include aphids and caterpillars. Flea beetles can be a problem too with field-sown crops. These can be controlled either by the use of chemicals or by organic means.

LEGUMES

For the purposes of this classification the legume group includes onions, leeks and spinach as well as peas and beans. This classification is appropriate because some of the general requirements of onions and leeks are similar to the genuine legumes. It is also common practice to group these crops for rotational purposes depending on the areas of each individual crop being grown. Lettuce and celery can also be included in this group if they are being grown outdoors and I will deal with them in detail in "Salad Crops" (see page 79).

Leguminous crops are generally known for their ability to "fix" free nitrogen in the soil due to the bacteria contained in the root nodules. This could indicate that they do not need either nitrogen fertilizers or the use of organic matter. In reality just the opposite is true.

All the crops in this group will benefit from dressings of farmyard manure of around twenty-eight tons per acre. The manure should be well rotted, particularly for onions. Farmyard manure can hinder root development in this crop. The organic matter will be beneficial in a number of ways. It will improve the soil structure, and all these crops like a deep, fertile, well-drained soil, as we have seen in Chapter 3. Organic matter will also help retain moisture since all legumes benefit from a moist soil. It will also go some way toward providing the nitrogen requirement of the crop. The ability of peas and beans to "fix" this nitrogen into the soil and, therefore, make it available for a following crop can be used to advantage in the rotation by following well-matured crops such as these with brassicas.

The soil for this group needs to be cultivated in autumn and the organic matter incorporated at this time. The pH of the soil should be between 6.3 and 7.5. If lime is needed (ideally, it should be included

Peas are grown in almost all parts of the United States with success.

in the rotation before brassicas), it can be applied after plowing. Subsequent cultivations should be aimed at producing a deeply worked soil with no compaction. This latter point is particularly relevant to onions and leeks as they do not have a branched rooting system; a deep root system with any compaction will restrict the root run and give a poor yield.

Peas

Peas of the right variety can be sown in autumn (October) and will normally produce a slightly earlier crop, with main sowings being made in March through May for succession. The selection of variety will depend on the site and the market the crop is destined for, as well as the intended harvest date. Sugarpeas (or mange-tout) may be good crops for the market garden as they are not grown widely and they command a good price.

Beans

There are many types of bean that can be grown. Grow only those that are best suited for the market outlet. Broad beans are eminently suitable for pick-your-own operations, as are peas. If growing for the wholesale markets, runner beans can be profitable if they can be trained economically; there is usually a good demand for quality runner beans even from the supermarkets. If growing for a retail outlet, pinched beans—that is, pinching out the tips of runner beans as they begin to "run"—will produce an earlier crop and hence command a high price; but having said that, the quality of pinched beans is often inferior to a trained crop. For the earliest crops, raising the plants under glass and transplanting them when frosts are over may give an early advantage.

French beans need to be sown when the soil is sufficiently warm. Drilling too early can result in disappointing germination and growth. In mid-range areas early May is best, though by using some form of protection this could be brought forward. Climbing French beans can be a more specialized crop and can perform well under cold glass.

Beans—always popular in the United States—are a viable product.

Weed control for peas and beans can be done both mechanically and chemically, and, of course, the land should be free of perennial weeds.

Pests and Diseases—These include the dreaded black bean aphid. Control measures for this common pest include removal of the soft growing shoots after the first pods have set. Late or delayed crops are the most susceptible. If using chemical control, care should be taken to avoid damaging pollinating bees. If five percent of plants in the southwest corner are infected, that is the time to instigate the spray program.

Chocolate spot can be a serious problem on broad beans. To reduce the risks, ensure that the site is well drained and neither too well sheltered nor too exposed. Autumn-sown crops are most susceptible, particularly in humid conditions. As with all groups, good hygiene must be practiced.

Halo blight and anthracnose can both be seed-borne. The latter problem can be serious, and if it occurs, no beans should be grown on that site for several years.

Onions and Leeks

Accurate drilling of all onion crops is essential for an even stand, and the seedbed should be prepared with this in mind to give a fine tilth. Spacing of rows will depend on the means of weed control to be used. Chemical weed control will allow closer spacings. No chemical herbicides should be applied between crop emergence and past crook stage.

This problem of weed control is also true for leeks, that is, no chemicals should be applied from germination to past crook stage. For this reason, leeks are often sown in a stale seedbed and then transplanted. This use of transplants makes weed control and crop management much easier. Both onions and leeks like a soil with a pH of 6.5 to 7.0 and the use of thirty tons per acre of well-rotted farmyard manure will be beneficial. Spacings, especially the widths between rows, will depend on the means of weed control being used.

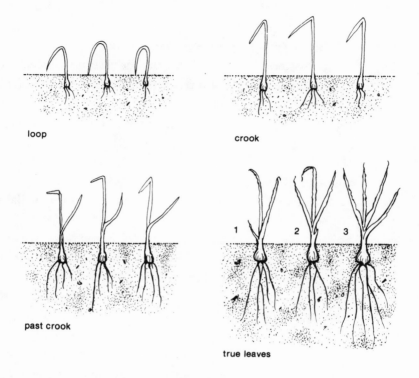

Figure 5.1. Stages of development of onion/leek seedlings.

Onions are normally lifted in late August and allowed to dry in the field (weather permitting), and then sold or stored for sale from September through March. To keep the crop later than March special storage areas are needed.

Leeks can be produced for harvest from late August through early May by the selection of suitable varieties. Timing of sowing will also affect the harvesting date.

Pests and Diseases—Pests are not normally a problem on onions and leeks, but eelworm and onion fly can sometimes be troublesome. Good hygiene and a rotation of a minimum of three years will help. For the fungal diseases, such as white rot and downy mildew, an even longer rotation should be practiced (five years minimum) and all infected plant and crop debris should be burnt. For details of chemicals to use it is best to contact your cooperative extension service.

Rust occurs on most leek crops; the most common source of infection is crop debris and volunteer plants in other parts of the holding.

Leek moth is also starting to be a problem in certain areas.

Spinach

This is another crop that can be included in this group. The benefits of having a well-manured soil for spinach include the available nitrogen and the added moisture retention—spinach is susceptible to drought. Spinach is a more specialized crop and should be grown only for a specific outlet. It is possible to crop from April until November from outdoor planting, and October until April under glass. Soil pH needs to be 6.5 to 7.0, and spinach should be grown on well-drained, moisture-retentive loams.

ROOTS

In this section we will consider carrots, parsnips, beets and potatoes though other specialized or unusual crops such as salsify and scorzenera would also come into this section.

Roots, in general, prefer a stone-free, light, sandy soil. Compaction can cause bent or forked roots, and for this reason a bed system is often used. Organic matter should not be incorporated for root crops—it will induce forking. In drier areas irrigation will be beneficial, though water should be applied consistently or the roots will split.

The basic nutritional requirements of this group of crops is for a low level of nitrogen but a relatively high level of phosphate and a medium level of potash. If we look briefly at this requirement in association with that of brassicas and legumes, we can see how the usual rotation of legumes, brassicas and roots has developed.

Growing carrots and other root plants under extensive floating film is becoming more popular. Due to the properties of the film, controlling pests and humidity are attractive.

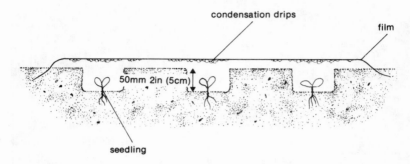

Figure 5.2. Recessed drills under floating film.

First year—farmyard manure and legumes
Second year—lime and brassicas
Third year—fertilizers and roots
Fourth year—farmyard manure and legumes

Carrots and Parsnips

Carrots grow best in sandy, stone-free soils or fen peats. The pH should be in the range of 5.8 to 6.8. The crop can be produced for sale at any time of the year, though to have roots for sale in June requires controlled storage and is probably beyond the means of a market garden. It should, however, be possible to produce fresh roots from under glass, if space is available. Roots for sale over the winter period (November through April or May) can either be stored under cover or in situ in the field. For the latter, a good cover of straw—fifteen inches deep—is needed and for late storage the straw should be covered with black polyethylene.

As has been stated, all efforts should be made to avoid soil compaction. A loose seedbed produced by a once-over pass is best. Fertilizers are best applied at plowing though nitrogen should be applied as a top dressing when the crop can utilize it. The crop is normally precision drilled to a given spacing. The exact spacing depends on the size of root required by the market outlet, as plant density has a major effect on the diameter of the root. Variety will depend on the sowing date and shape required. If you are not sure what variety to grow, consult your local extension office for a list of many vegetable varieties and their uses, which may be a useful alternative source of information to seed catalogs. The crop responds well to the use of floating films (see Chapter 7), but if using such techniques to gain early production, ensure the film is removed at the six to seven true-leaf stage. If using film, it is usual to sow the drills in hollows to keep the seedlings away from the condensation on the film.

The above details are similar for parsnips and carrots. Both these crops are normally marketed in twenty-eight-pound bags or nets. There may be marketing opportunities with catering establishments for baby carrots and even baby carrots with foliage over a larger season.

Pests and Diseases—The first one that springs to mind is, of course, carrot-root fly. This pest is very like cabbage-root fly. It produces three generations in most seasons, the first at the end of May, the second in mid-August and the third at the end of September. In high-risk areas, the use of chemicals will not give complete control. The real key to preventing this problem is isolation. If you are lucky enough to be at least two miles from any other carrots, parsnips, celery or parsley, you may not have a major problem. Sheltered fields are also more susceptible to carrot-root fly damage. In fact, the first generation can be missed by timing sowings so that the crop emerges after the risk of infection is past. It is the second generation that causes the real problems. Attempts at chemical control can be made by the use of granules at drilling and sprays in mid-season. There are a few products reputed to have some resistance to carrot-root fly. For the organic grower, covering the crop with a material such as Agrinet at high-risk times may help, and smell-hiding compounds are said to be useful as well. The third generation is only likely to cause problems in crops stored in the field after early October.

The fungal disease of cavity spot can cause problems but can be controlled chemically. Violet root rot is a much more serious soil-borne fungal disease, and if this is found on your land carrots should not be grown for ten to fifteen years. Mayweed and chickweed are also susceptible to violet root rot.

With parsnips, the main problems are canker and carrot-root fly. The variety Avon Reister is resistant to all forms of canker and should be grown where the disease is a problem. Other cultural methods which may help include good drainage, closer spacings, later sowings and earthing up in summer. The use of clean seed is also recommended.

Beetroot

Beetroot is only really worth growing for an established fresh market outlet—returns on this crop can be low. It is normally sown from April to July, though there is a tendency on the early sowings to bolt (run to seed). This is due to a combination of low temperatures and long days. Some varieties, such as Voltardy, have resistance to this problem. When drilling, if using a precision drill, the use of rubbed seed will improve the number of singles sown. If mechanical weed control is to be used, the incorporation of some radish seed will enable the rows to be seen, as beetroot is slow to germinate. Spacing, both within the row and of rows, will depend on the size of roots required by the market outlet. Soil conditions should be as for the other roots. Irrigation is necessary for top quality due to beetroot's shallow rooting and easy wilting in dry weather. The normal harvest period is from July to November and the crop can be stored for winter sales using a clamp made of straw bales.

Potatoes

The other main root crop is the potato. In many intensive market gardens there may not be room to produce potatoes economically, but there may be marketing opportunities that cannot be ignored. Specializing in salad potatoes or unusual varieties such as

Pink Fir Apple may be worth consideration. Potatoes are often used as "ground breakers," as they like an organic-matter-enriched soil and are often used as a first crop in a rotation.

Always use certified seed; never use twice-kept seed. The seed should be chitted early (left in a cool, dry, light place to develop sprouts), and hand or machine planting can be done. Potatoes prefer a soil that has had minimal cultivation, with a pH between 5.5 and 6.5. The crop is responsive to phosphates, and potash levels should be kept low. Earlies should be planted in early March when the soil temperature is above 39°F.

Weed control is only necessary until the crop covers the ground, and it can be done either chemically or mechanically by ridging.

Potatoes are very responsive to irrigation. A minimum amount of one inch of water per week is required, either from rain or irrigation, from the tuber marbling stage. Harvesting can be by hand or by machine but potatoes should never be dropped more than six inches.

Pests and Diseases—These include blight, scab, wire worm and nematodes. Blight can infect any crop after a "blight period" of warm damp days. This disease can only survive on living plant material, so hygiene can help. If it does occur do not irrigate and if tubers are sufficiently large destroy the haulm to prevent spread. Chemical sprays only delay the inevitable but may take the crop harvest. Scab can be a problem, particularly in alkaline or limed soils, but the use of irrigation will help to control it. Wireworms are usually only a problem if the crop is following permanent pasture. Nematodes or eelworms can be a problem and the use of a good long rotation will help prevent the buildup of this pest.

Alternative Cropping Ideas

There are some other vegetables that can be considered suitable market garden crops. These include the marrow family, sweet corn and more unusual vegetables such as kohlrabi, fennel, scorzenera and celeriac.

There is nothing like the taste of fresh sweet corn. It is a favorite among many market garden customers and is ideal for pick-your-own enterprises.

Marrows, courgettes and the less common squashes and pumpkins all like a soil rich in organic matter, and the ability to irrigate the crop can be an advantage. When considering these crops, the areas grown should be evaluated carefully, for some crops may take up large areas (pumpkins, etc.), while others have a high labor input (especially courgettes, which really need harvesting on a daily basis to prevent the fruit becoming too large).

Sweet corn, like beans, lends itself to the pick-your-own enterprise. This product suits the smaller grower and can give good returns.

SALAD CROPS

This group of crops could be very important to the market garden. Once again, crops that are grown on an extensive scale such as

Lettuce seedlings can be grown in peat blocks.

lettuce and celery should perhaps be grown only if for a specific outlet, as market prices and volumes make the economics of these crops questionable. More unusual varieties of lettuce such as Little Gem, the endive and red varieties may be suitable crops. Round or butterhead lettuce can be produced outdoors from May to October.

Plants are normally raised in peat blocks and transplanted. Since the growing period is relatively short, continuity can be achieved on a relatively small area. Crisp or iceberg lettuce takes a little longer, and cropping of cos types is more restricted. Lettuce is often used as a "bread and butter" crop in many modern market gardens, but be prepared to plow in some crops if market prices make harvesting uneconomic.

Lettuce is also susceptible to a wide range of pests and diseases, but chemical controls are readily available.

Celery, as just mentioned, is possibly not a crop for the market garden but can be grown successfully outdoors using the self-blanching types. Irrigation is a necessity for this crop, as is a good, rich moisture-retentive soil.

Radishes and salad onions can easily be grown on small areas and in continuity. I know of some market gardens that have specialized in these crops and have been very successful in supplying national supermarket chains.

For early production of all these crops, light land with a southern exposure is best and irrigation a must to reach the quality standards now being demanded.

PROTECTED CROPPING

There is quite a range of crops that can be grown under protection for most outlets. For these purposes glass is best, but good crops can be grown under polyethylene . The crops that can be grown in this way include tomatoes, cucumbers, peppers, aubergines, melons, lettuces, radishes and celery. These crops can be divided for ease into trained and untrained (or ground) crops.

When growing under protective structures of glass or polyethylene great attention must be given to the soil. Most protected structures are cropped intensively, and this can cause problems if care is not taken. The soil structure needs to be improved to maintain a good root zone, so the regulation addition of organic matter will be beneficial, as will regular timing. Under protected structures, regular liming will be necessary as the use of fertilizers, liquid feeds and farmyard manure will all acidify the soil, even in hard-water areas. The pH should, therefore, be checked regularly and adjusted as necessary. Regular subsoiling and the occasional use of deep cultivations will also be useful in extending the root zone.

One result of this intensive cropping may be a buildup of soil-borne pests and disease, especially as rotation is often impractical under protection. This could mean that the soil will need some form of sterilization at regular intervals which can be done either by chemicals or by steam sterilization. It is now possible to buy or perhaps hire some mobile steam generators which should make this viable, certainly for small areas.

The use of poly-tunnels has become a viable means of controlled growing. This one has installed irrigation and doors at each end for ventilation.

Quick coupling to allow liquid feeding via overhead spraylines is an effective way of delivering nutrients evenly over a growing space.

Two other factors need to be mentioned since they play a vital role in protected cropping: ventilation and irrigation. Ideally, the ventilation area in a greenhouse should be between one-third and one-sixth of the floor area. It is often smaller, which can cause problems during the season. Irrigation systems also need to be good and well maintained. A crop of summer lettuce under glass will soon show up any weaknesses in an overhead irrigation system. It can also be of great advantage to be able to liquid feed via both an overhead irrigation system and a low-level or trickle system.

Finally, crop supporting wires need to be substantial, well maintained and securely attached to strong ends of the structure. I have heard of a greenhouse that had grown tomatoes successfully for many years, but when a crop of cucumbers was grown, the ends of the greenhouse were pulled in! One tip: Keep crop support wires in as short a section as practical for two reasons. First, they are not supporting such a weight, and second, if they do break they are easier to repair. Mine was 150 feet long when it snapped!

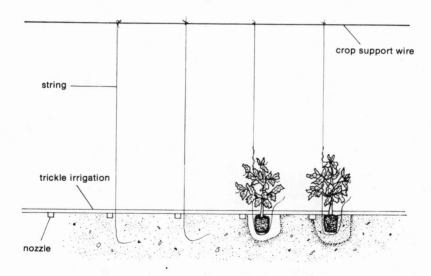

Figure 5.3. Stringing and planting tomatoes. The string is placed under the rootball.

Tomatoes

Tomatoes are probably the single largest crop grown under protection, but from a market garden point of view they will probably only be grown for sale at a local retail point. There are several types that can be grown these days: the normal round types, beef or marmande types, cherry tomatoes and even plum and yellow tomatoes.

The training system is similar for all types. Unheated crops are usually planted in April when the glass will keep out any late frosts. The plants should have the first few flowers open at planting. I liked to prepare the house fully before planting to facilitate easy care later in the growing process. After soil preparations, the trickle irrigation was laid. The individual strings were then tied to the wire, the length being about eighteen to twenty-four inches longer than that needed to touch the floor.

When we planted, the string was passed under the rootball. The tension was sufficient to hold the string, especially as I gave the first twist at planting. I found that this procedure meant that I did not have to return to the house for training for possibly two weeks until the plants had grown sufficiently to warrant twisting around the string and side-shooting. I also removed as many side-shoots as possible at planting.

All watering was done by trickle irrigation and feeding started after about three weeks, depending on crop growth. The crop should be sprayed over with a high-pressure water jet between 11 A.M. and 1 P.M. to aid setting of early fruit. Some growers use an "electric bee" for this. The crop should be deleafed to aid air circulation and enable fruit to be seen for picking. If growing cherry tomatoes, leave approximately three to four feet of foliage on the plant as you will be picking from the first and eighth truss at the same time!

On reaching the support wires, the plants can either be stopped (that is, the tip pinched out) or trained along the top wire or across the patch. Stopping should take place six weeks before it is intended to remove the crop to enable all the fruit to ripen.

When growing cherry tomatoes, such as Gardener's Delight, certain modifications to a normal feed regime are needed. To gain maximum flavor, use about half the volume of water of a normal crop and always use a high potash liquid feed. Care is needed to balance the water and feed requirements to control the crop. Too much water and it will go wild; too little and it will stop growing altogether.

Pests and Diseases—The main pests and diseases for the crop are whitefly, red spider mite and botrytis. I have managed to control the pests successfully by biological means. Of course, they can be controlled by chemical means. Resistance can be built up, so use at least three different insecticides. Alternating both systems can help.

Red spider mites prefer hot, dry conditions, so dampening the crop can help reduce the numbers. Having said that, a damp atmosphere is ripe for an infestation of botrytis. This can be limited to a greater or lesser degree by cultural methods. Regular deleafing, general hygiene and good ventilation all help to reduce the incidence, as will ensuring that the crop is dry at the end of the day. It is important to control botrytis—even at low levels of infection "ghost spotting" can occur on the fruit and detract from its quality.

Other diseases can be a problem, especially some soil-borne ones such as fusarium. If they become a major problem, it may not be possible to cure them by sterilization, and the crop will have to be grown in grow bags instead.

Cucumbers

Traditionally, cucumbers were grown on straw bales. This practice is not necessary for short-term crops, but a soil rich in organic matter will be of real benefit. Cucumbers are gross feeders and require large amounts of nitrogen. They come into cropping in a relatively short period and can be quite prolific. A good crop can be grown in the older types of greenhouses, but remember that the crop can be heavy and support wires need to be strong. Plant them a little later than tomatoes when the soil is warmer. If trying to produce over a long period, replanting in mid-season or interplanting could ensure continuity of supplies. The use of all-female flowering varieties will eliminate the problem of bitter fruit. For maximum weight do not let any fruit develop on the bottom two feet of the main stem. The plants can be trained either as cordons with the fruit on the main stem or on short laterals, or by the umbrella method, that is a single main stem with several branches at the top.

Pests and Diseases—Pest and diseases are very similar to tomatoes, but extra care is required when using chemicals, as cucumbers can be susceptible. Whitefly is probably the biggest problem as a pest and mildew as a disease. The mildew is a powdery type which prefers a dry atmosphere, so increasing the humidity will help; however, this can encourage botrytis if overdone.

Peppers and Aubergines

I have grouped these two crops together because their basic requirements are very similar. They should not be planted out too early as they like to go into a warm soil, and our experience shows there is little to be gained from planting before the end of April when no heat is available for the crop.

Some form of training is required to support the plants. It can range from a single cane or single string, like tomatoes, to four strings to support each branch. One advantage of these crops is that they do not have such a large labor requirement as tomatoes or cucumbers, since training and picking only needs to be done every ten to fourteen days.

Feed requirements are basically a warm rich soil and liquid feed, with a medium nitrogen feed at each watering. Blossom drop can be caused by uneven watering and the crops benefit from damping down. The first "king fruit" on peppers may need to be removed as it can often become wedged between the branches.

Pests and Diseases—Red spider mite can be a problem, particularly with aubergines. Caterpillars can be damaging in a crop of peppers and can be difficult to spray as the foliage is so dense.

Lettuce

Lettuce can be grown all the year round under glass, though careful selection of varieties is required. Spacing varies but is most commonly nine by nine inches. Lettuce requires a good rich soil with a pH of 6.5. Soil conductivity should be low and, if lettuce is following a crop such as tomatoes, flooding may be necessary to reduce the level of salts in the soil.

Hygiene is important with continuous production, and all crop debris should be removed from the greenhouse. Regular sterilization is needed. Ventilation of the crop is critical, and air movement can help to reduce the problems of glassiness and will help prevent rots. Good overhead irrigation is required; if there is any unevenness in the pattern of the nozzles, this will soon become apparent and an uneven crop will result.

Paths should be kept to a minimum, but all parts of the crop should be accessible for spraying with crop protection chemicals. On my own holding, I used a motorized knapsack sprayer with all insecticides and fungicides, which proved very effective on any crop.

Care should be taken when harvesting the crop, and all harvesting should be finished by 10 A.M. in summer to prevent a buildup of field heat in the product. This applies to all leafy crops, as it is field heat that reduces the shelf life of the produce.

Pests and Diseases—Many pests and diseases can affect lettuce. Continuous production can greatly increase the risks of problems occurring. Good hygiene must always be practiced; any rubbish heaps must be located well away from production areas. The most common problems include aphids, botrytis, tip burn and a range of bottom rots. With fungal diseases, keeping some air movement around the crops and watering only in the mornings will help reduce the instances. Mildew can also be a problem and resistant varieties should be grown where applicable. A range of chemicals should always be used to prevent a buildup of resistant strains.

Celery

Celery can be grown indoors for harvest during May and June. For the early crop, heat or some form of frost protection is needed. When propagating celery plants for early production ensure that they do not get checked and are propagated at relatively high temperatures, as this helps to prevent bolting. Once again, the crop has a high demand for water, so a good irrigation system is essential.

The crop benefits from the incorporation of high levels of farmyard manure prior to planting although this can cause problems with slugs and weeds. Both can be controlled chemically, but if using herbicides under glass great care is required. This practice is not normally recommended.

The crop will require feeding with nitrogen, either by using a nitrogen liquid feed at every watering via the overhead irrigation, ensuring it is washed off the foliage, or by hand. If using the latter system, a watering can with a short length of hose on the end of the spout makes an ideal applicator. Two solid dressings should be applied, one when the crop is established and one at the last possible time the crop can be walked over. The fertilizer only needs to be applied to every other row, but take care it does not touch the plants. With self-blanching crops a nine-by-nine inch spacing is suitable.

The main labor input on celery is at harvest. All the crop will need to be cut in a relatively short time for top quality.

Pests and Diseases—The crop is relatively free of pests and diseases but aphids can be a problem, especially around any weeds that appear. Slugs can be controlled by adding slug pellets to solid top dressings or at planting time.

Sclerotinia disease can be a problem; if it occurs, infected plants should be removed carefully and destroyed and the soil sterilized after harvest. Once on a holding, it cannot easily be eradicated but can be kept to acceptable levels. The other major problem is leaf spot. This usually comes in on infected seed or plants or via the water supply. Regular spraying can control it, but initially removal of infected plants is advised. Outdoors and even in a greenhouse it can be spread by rabbits running along the rows!

Radishes and Salad Onions

These can also be grown under glass both all year round and to extend the season early and late. Other possible crops include calabrese, endive and kohlrabi. These are alternatives to winter lettuce.

HERBS

Herb growing now has a new lease on life with the change in eating habits and the rise in alternative medicine. Many people have seen herb growing as a new area for production. Appraise the marketing opportunities carefully before taking the plunge. Herbs can be marketed as a fresh product or dried.

For production, a good, rich soil free of perennial weeds is required. With herb crops, weed control needs to be carefully considered. It may not be possible to use chemicals because the market

Herb growers have a long tradition in growing and selling direct to the consumer. Herbs have been used for a variety of purposes for thousands of years.

Strawberries are very popular with the consumers, but present special problems for the gardener. Here strawberries are grown through plastic mulch.

demands an organic product. There is also a lack of approved chemicals for use on the range of herbs being grown.

The crops will be labor intensive to harvest and need to be cut at the correct stage to maximize returns. Any drying must be done carefully to retain the aromatic oils and may require special drying areas.

Having said all this, a market garden specializing in herb production could be very profitable, so it may be worth consideration.

FRUIT

Extensive growing of fruit may not be included in the field of market gardening, but traditionally market gardens did grow some fruit.

Soft fruit (strawberries, raspberries, currants, etc.) lend themselves to the pick-your-own enterprise and make a welcome addition to the farm shop outlet. If you are planning a pick-your-own enterprise, consider the potential market and the number of customers when defining possible areas of each crop.

Strawberries are the most popular crop. Only clean, certified plants should be used and beds will need replanting about every five years. There can be problems with strawing the crop and trying to keep runners under control, though I have heard of one pick-your-own grower who used the "matted bed" system.

Raspberries, blackberries and hybrid berries all need suitable support systems and regular maintenance. Currants and gooseberries are not as popular, so grow relatively small areas of those at first.

Melons are not widely grown commercially as yields can be low, making the economics of the crop questionable. Where they have been grown for farm shop sales, the response from the public has been excellent and they may well be a crop to consider. Culturally they are similar to cucumbers and will need some form of protection, that is, a greenhouse, tunnel or cold frame. They will require a higher level of potash to ensure flavor in the fruit and more time in training as the fruits themselves may need supporting.

Top fruits such as apples, pears and plums are really beyond the scope of a modern market garden, but may make a welcome addition to farm shop lines.

There may be a good opening for an organic pick-your-own garden in many places.

OTHER CROPPING IDEAS

There are some other lines that can be sold via the holding's own retail outlet and can be produced with minimal specialist equipment. These include bedding plants, some shrubs and potted plants. However, all these are specialist areas and not really market garden crops.

CHAPTER 6

Machinery and Equipment

*I*n this chapter we will look at the range of machinery that is available to the modern market gardener. The actual equipment bought and used by the grower will depend on several factors. First and foremost of these will be money. Machinery is expensive, though by careful matching of machine to job, great savings in time and costs can be made.

Other factors to be considered are the range of crops being grown and the soil type one has to deal with in the operation. There is not space in a book such as this to go into details of individual machines and makes, but by considering various options the grower should be able to make the best choice of equipment for his or her own situation.

PRIME MOVERS

This is perhaps an unusual heading but in reality quite logical, for it is in this section that the tractor must be considered. The choice of these prime movers was limited in the past, but in recent years the range of small and compact tractors has increased dramatically. The modern, compact Japanese or Soviet tractors make an ideal tool for the market gardener. There is also a wide range of implements available for these compact tractors, and their small size and maneuverability make them ideal for use under glass as well as in the field. The smaller standard tractors are also versatile machines and are much more readily available secondhand, although they are expensive. When buying secondhand compact tractors, especially the early models, check the range of implements available. Some of the early models only take specific equipment.

Another prime mover is the Rototiller. Several types can make

Prime mover I. A modern small tractor is ideally suited to a market garden.

quite a wide range of implements, including trailers. On my holding I used a Honda Rototiller as my main power unit. By changing the rotors for wheels, it pulled a trailer and moved over 250 tons of farmyard manure and many thousands of boxes of produce around the holding over seven years. It was not legal for road use—it had no brakes (it was a flat holding!)—but it did save the legs.

A subsoiler is used for pan busting.

A tractor-mounted Rototiller is ideal for larger operations.

A pedestrian-operated Rototiller is more likely to be used by most smaller market gardeners. It also may be preferable for working depth and conditioning.

CULTIVATION EQUIPMENT

There is a vast range of both types of makes of cultivation equipment and much of the general equipment can be bought readily on the secondhand market. Plows are the major primary cultivation tools of the farmer and grower. The size and type required will depend on the power of the tractor pulling it. It may be possible to use a contractor or a neighboring farmer to plow the relatively small area needed. The timing of these operations can be critical and it may be advisable to do one's own work.

A subsoiler is a useful piece of equipment to have access to (see Chapter 3, page 32). Once again, match the size to the power available.

The range of secondary cultivators available includes rigid and spring tine types, disc and other harrows, all of which can be useful and should be matched to soil type and conditions. Used correctly on reasonable soil conditions they produce a workable tilth.

The mode of action of tined cultivators produces a crumb structure that can help prevent capping or surface panning on susceptible soils. It may take several passes of the cultivator to obtain a good tilth and this can increase compaction. Powdered cultivators, such as rotary harrows, can reduce the number of passes required but need a tractor with a relatively large power output to drive them. This may take them beyond the means of the market gardener.

The piece of equipment most commonly used is the Rototiller. Since its introduction, it has revolutionized ground preparation. It chops up weeds and crop debris, breaks up soils and prepares a soil bed all in one pass. It can be obtained in all sizes to match a tractor of any power output. It sounds like a panacea for every ground preparation problem, but this is not so. When a Rototiller is used without due care and thought, real damage can be done to the soil structure. It is the one piece of cultivation equipment, if not the only one, that can create a "cultivation pan" and destroy the vital crumb structure in the soil by its working. If used correctly, however, a Rototiller can solve most

A steerage hoe, for interrow work, is essential for good weed control.

cultivation problems. Care should be taken to match rotor speed with ground speed and the soil type and conditions of the day. Remember, fastest ground speed plus slowest rotor speed to produce an acceptable tilth will not cause any soil damage. So exercise caution and only use one when the soil moisture content is at a suitable level.

Rototillers can be mounted on tractors either offset or parallel. An offset machine will remove the tractor wheelings on one side and hence wheelings can be removed from the field. The centrally mounted versions can be readily adapted as a bed-forming machine and are best used when a bed system of production is being used. It is possible to fit "pan buster" tines to follow the tractor wheels to reduce compaction. Some machines have been developed that have a series of small rotors that can be used for interrow work, but these specialized machines are expensive. To prevent a "cultivation pan," the depth of use should be varied, or use tines on soils that are sensitive to panning.

WEED CONTROL MACHINES

Most weed control equipment relies on the hoe principle. Blades or tines of various types and designs are attached to a tool frame and pulled through the soil. Like any hoe, they should cut the weeds off just below the soil surface. To make sure of this, the blades need to be checked and replaced regularly. These types of hoe can be used for interrow work and, for this purpose, steerable hoes are less likely to cause crop damage.

Recently, the upsurge of interest in organic growing has fueled development of other types of weed control as an alternative to spraying chemicals. Two developments that have come out of this are modern flame guns and brush weeders. Flame guns can be fueled by paraffin or gas; brush weeders use contrarotating brushes to scrub up the weeds. They actually do this without stirring up the soil too much or bringing more weed seeds to the surface, ready to germinate.

Row spacings need to take the tractors' wheels into account when using tractor-driven hoes or weeders. Bed systems can help reduce the potential for compaction and drainage from the tractor's wheels. Compact tractors are unable to leave their wheels extended to give as good a bed width as full-size tractors. The ground clearance of the tractor will be important because the vehicle passes over the crop.

For small areas nothing can beat the good old hand hoe. There have been several developments, though, the main one being some form of double-sided blade so that the hoe will cut on both the push and pull strokes. In between the two extremes, hoe and cultivator tines can be fitted to some pedestrian-controlled Rototillers.

SPRAYERS

There is quite a range of sprayers suitable for use on the market garden, from small knapsack types to tractor-mounted types. A good sprayer is just as necessary to an organic holding for using organic materials such as soft soap. All sprayers should be regularly maintained to ensure they are applying the correct amount of chemical safely. Blocked or damaged nozzles can cause pollution and damage to crops by giving an uneven spread.

In an attempt to prevent crop damage, it is a good idea to have one sprayer for crop protection chemicals and one sprayer for herbicides. This prevents damage to crops due to incomplete washing out after herbicide use. On my own holding I used a standard hand-pumped four-gallon knapsack for herbicide applications and a motorized air-blast knapsack sprayer for all crop protection work. I found this latter worked effectively both indoors and out, giving good coverage of the crop, especially to the undersides of the leaves where most pests congregate. It was used with success on a wide range of crops, from lettuce to cucumbers and tomatoes to celery.

The "turbair" system works well under glass, though the range of specially formulated chemicals is limited. The next stage upward from the knapsack is one of the barrow types of sprayer. These carry a larger tank and cover a wider area of ground. After that, there are tractor-mounted sprayers. These can be boom sprayers and may be adapted to enable a hand lance to be attached for spraying in the greenhouse.

Great care should be exercised in calibrating your sprayer. It is essential to get the application rate correct, as too much can cause

Figure 6.1. Rototiller with marker drams.

crop damage, is expensive and can pollute the environment. Too little, on the other hand, is ineffective and a waste of time and money.

FERTILIZER SPREADERS

I have yet to locate a suitable pedestrian-operated fertilizer spreader for use on a market garden. There are several on the market that can be either trailed behind or mounted on the compact tractors. Most are of the spinning-disc type or the oscillating-spout type. Once again, good calibration is needed to ensure the correct amount is applied. This can be done either by spreading a known weight of fertilizer and measuring the area covered or by collecting the fertilizer spread over a known area. The spreader will require calibrating for each material used. This sounds like a real chore, but if done properly, it will ensure economic use of fertilizers and, combined with regular maintenance of the spreader, will ensure that no problems occur with spreading or wastage.

Many market gardeners use the trusted "bucket and chuck it" system. When applying fertilizers by hand, it is best to split the dressing and apply the second part at right angles to the first to be certain of an even coverage of ground. With a little practice it is amazing how quick and accurate application by hand can become.

SEED DRILLS

Precision drills, which sow a seed a specific distance from its neighbor, are ideally suited to outdoor vegetable production. They are economical with seed and can be obtained as single, hand-pushed units or in more sophisticated forms, up to multirow, tractor-mounted versions.

There is a range of seed-metering devices available, the most common being cell wheels and perforated belts. Both can be obtained in a range of spacings and for a range of seed sizes. When using precision drills it is wise to use graded seed.

Cheaper, less accurate types of drill are available. To some extent the seed drill is in the process of being almost phased out as more and more vegetable plants are being raised and transplanted using the module system.

PLANTING MACHINES

Planting machines range from fully automatic machines capable of handling large numbers of plants per hour to some basic devices that only mark out the ground.

Two of the basic types of machines may be suitable for use on a market garden. One is the tractor-mounted type of cabbage planter that has been around for a long time and can be found secondhand. These machines usually have a system of fingers or discs to hold the plants, and they can be used and adapted for a wide range of plants. The modern module planters are probably out of reach financially for the normal small market garden but there may be secondhand machines available.

A third type of planting machine available is the lettuce planter. This consists of a pair of rollers on a common axle on which are placed bands with marker lumps at a regular spacing. Behind the rollers is a frame with seats for the operators. A rack at the front and back on which trays of plants can be stacked completes the machine. It can be driven either by a small gas engine or by an electric motor, and there is a definite knack in steering them. With two skilled planters on a machine of this type, up to twenty thousand plants per day can be inserted. The bands can be moved to allow different spacings to be achieved.

If these machines prove too expensive, cheaper alternatives are available; I had some "drums" made up to fit on the Honda Rototiller at a reasonable cost. This device marked out and, if the soil conditions were reasonable, made a hole in which to drop the block-grown plant. I have used this system—and a planting machine—for round lettuces, icebergs, celery, cabbages and leeks, and it could be used for any block, or even module-raised plants. A hand-pushed roller with lumps can also be used.

HARVESTING EQUIPMENT

Some special harvesting equipment has been developed, but for the market gardener an elevator type of root lifter and/or a lifting blade will be more suitable. Perhaps the best, and certainly the cheapest, harvesting machine is the pick-your-own customer! There are other machines that in reality are aids to harvesting. In this group I will include such equipment as the lettuce elevator that can be used on a wide range of crops and can lessen damage and ease the grading and packing operations.

GRADING AND PACKING EQUIPMENT

With certain crops some form of grader will be necessary to ensure conformity to certain market standards. Tomatoes are an obvious crop. Once again, the small area of a particular crop may make the economics of such grading equipment a farce. One answer may be to join a local marketing cooperative. Other ideas have run on the lines of a mobile packing station that can be organized around an elevator. Another system is to have a large netted "basket" at the front into which the cutters drop the produce. The packer then takes the produce out, weighs it if necessary and packs it in the appropriate box. Pallet-wrapping devices may also be useful if produce is being moved on pallets.

A cold store is well worth considering. It will prolong the shelf life of the produce harvested, as it will remove the field heat as soon as possible and will enable the produce to reach the customer in better condition than would otherwise be possible. There are three ways of procuring a cold store. They can be purchased as a unit, existing buildings can be converted or an old refrigerated truck back or container can be used. The latter needs to be adjusted to maintain a temperature of about 39°F. When considering the possibilities, a straight-through system should be adopted if possible. This enables freshly harvested produce to come in one side and cooled produce to leave the other. The use of a cold store will be a necessity if supplying a multiple chain or a marketing organization supplying similar customers.

TRANSPORTATION

On-holding transport

Some form of transport is needed to move things around on the holding. If a tractor is available, a trailer and a transport box will be extremely useful. Another common means of transport is a tractor-mounted pallet lift. Standard pallets or pallet bins can be used to move a range of objects, and, when using them, some means of moving them round the packing shed or cold store will be needed. It may also be necessary to have some means of loading directly onto trucks.

Some form of personal transport may save a lot of walking time. An old van, pickup or station wagon can be used but may be limited to dry days. I knew of one holding where the grower used a scooter to get around. A modern all-terrain, three- or four-wheeled vehicle would be ideal but perhaps may not fully justifiable.

Off-holding transportation

Obviously, this form of transportation must be road legal. It may be possible to use the same vehicle for on- and off-holding transport. What determines the best mode of transport is the use to which it will be put. If you have to transport produce to customers, a van of some sort may be most suitable; if delivery is to the local packhouse just down the road, a tractor and trailer or pallet lift may be adequate. If the produce is collected directly from the holding, transportation may not be needed.

IRRIGATION EQUIPMENT

Irrigation is vital in order to obtain the maximum yield from your land. In reality, most crops will benefit from irrigation at some time—when sowing or transplanting, to ensure maximum growth, to aid harvesting and even for frost protection. A plant that suffers no water stress will reach harvest more quickly and have a greater weight than one that needs to struggle to survive. The judicious use of water will help to obtain ideal soil moisture levels when cultivation operations are to be done. For intensive crop production in most areas of the

An outdoor sprinkler nozzle gives a fine spray.

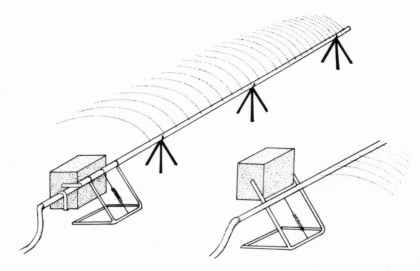

Figure 6.2. Bucket oscillator and sprayline. The bucket fills and empties, which turns the spraylines.

country, irrigation is a necessity as soil moisture deficiency can build up to levels that will reduce plant growth in seventeen years out of twenty.

There is a range of systems available to the grower, and the advantage and disadvantages of each need to be assessed and matched to individual requirements. The main considerations other than cost are droplet size and the area to be covered. Droplet size is important— it can have a marked effect on the soil. Some types of soil can be prone to capping, particularly those with poor structure or low levels of organic matter. The effect of large droplets falling on the soil is to pulverize the surface, destroying the crumb structure. This can happen to the extent that it can prevent the germination of seeds. Those types of irrigation that apply water in large drops are best suited to established crops. Finer types of irrigation are best for seedbed work and on sandy soils. Large droplet size has the advantage that it is less likely to be blown by wind, and therefore can give a more even spread over the field.

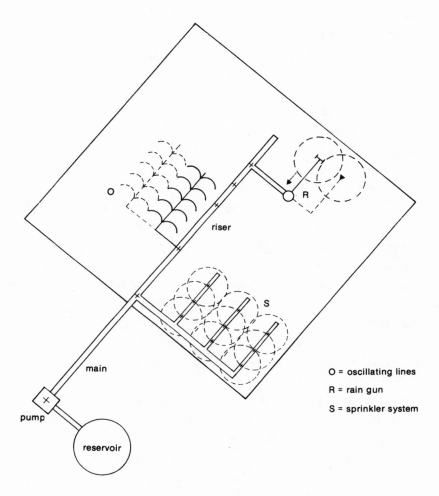

Figure 6.3. Layout and comparative areas covered by oscillating spraylines, sprinklers and rain guns.

When choosing an irrigation system, the area that will be irrigated and the frequency of irrigation need to be considered. The other major factor is to match pump output—both in terms of pressure and volume of water—to the irrigation type. Rain-gun-type irrigators require a relatively high pressure (approximately seventy psi) to operate effectively, whereas oscillating spraylines can work effectively at much lower pressures.

Thought must be given to the water source when planning an irrigation system. Mains water is expensive and must have a ball valve or some other arrangement to prevent "suck back" into the water supply. This is imperative if liquid feeding is to be done. Wells and streams may provide good sources of supply in some areas. Check with the local water authority. Water rights is a sensitive issue throughout most of the United States.

Having located a suitable source of water, some form of reservoir will be needed. These can be sunk into the ground and may need lining with butyl rubber to ensure they are watertight. Alternatively, storage tanks—also lined—can be erected. A pump of suitable output will be needed; these can be electric or motor driven. It is possible to get pumps to fit onto the takeoff on the tractor. This could cause problems when the tractor is needed for other operations at the same times.

Some form of main pipe will be needed; when laying this, it is best buried below normal cultivation depth and ideally below subsoiling depth to minimize damage. Always use the largest size of main you can afford as future requirements cannot always be assessed accurately. There is nothing worse than having to replace a main with one of a larger bore two years after laying it. The pressure drop in large-bore pipes is also less over a given distance. The system should be as simple as possible, with minimum bends as pressure is lost due to friction each time it changes direction.

TYPES OF IRRIGATION

Oscillating Spraylines

These produce a relatively small droplet and are ideal for use on seedbeds. There are two basic types available: bucket and pump versions.

The system illustrated in Figure 6.2 is mobile; it does take some time to move, but I was able to move one 150 feet to the next site in about twenty minutes. This system can be used on most field crops effectively. The spray can be sensitive to the wind and frequency of pathways may need to be taken into account. If using this sytem, ensure that the water supply is well filtered. Often weed seeds and other debris can easily block the small jets and result in uneven application.

Portable Grid Systems

These can be purchased either in rigid plastic or aluminum pipes. Combing this with self-sealing risers enables the spray heads to be moved much more quickly than the previous system. It is also possible to move the sprinklers while the system is operating, but you do tend to have a shower. If finances allow, the purchase of sufficient pipes so they can be put down for the season and only removed for cultivations, etc., is recommended. The droplet size will depend on the nozzle type.

The most common form is the periot type or "ticking nozzle," where the droplets will normally be medium-sized. They will not be too sensitive to wind but can cause some capping on certain soils.

Rain Guns

Included here are the reel type of irrigators. These can be found in a range of sizes and capacities, some of which are suitable for the market garden. They can be moved relatively easily from one site to another but require a good pipe pressure. They also cover a wider area. The droplet size will be large and could cause problems, but will be the least sensitive to wind.

When using irrigation, the amount of water being applied should be checked occasionally. This can easily be done by placing a rain gauge on the area being irrigated. It is also beneficial to try to irrigate either late in the day or early in the morning. This enables the soil to absorb the maximum amount of water and reduces the losses from evaporation. Watering during the heat of the day in summer can cause crop damage from scorch, and it will take much longer to wet the soil effectively.

pipes. Combing this with self-sealing risers enables the spray heads to be moved much more quickly than the previous system. It is also possible to move the sprinklers while the system is operating, but you do tend to have a shower. If finances allow, the purchase of sufficient pipes so they can be put down for the season and only removed for cultivations, etc., is recommended. The droplet size will depend on the nozzle type.

The most common form is the periot type or "ticking nozzle," where the droplets will normally be medium-sized. They will not be too sensitive to wind but can cause some capping on certain soils.

Rain Guns

Included here are the reel type of irrigators. These can be found in a range of sizes and capacities, some of which are suitable for the market garden. They can be moved relatively easily from one site to another but require a good pipe pressure. They also cover a wider area. The droplet size will be large and could cause problems, but will be the least sensitive to wind.

When using irrigation, the amount of water being applied should be checked occasionally. This can easily be done by placing a rain gauge on the area being irrigated. It is also beneficial to try to irrigate either late in the day or early in the morning. This enables the soil to absorb the maximum amount of water and reduces the losses from evaporation. Watering during the heat of the day in summer can cause crop damage from scorch, and it will take much longer to wet the soil effectively.

CHAPTER 7

Protective Structures and Films

*T*he use of protection, be it glass or polyethylene, can extend the range of crops grown and the harvesting season. There cannot be many holdings that do not use some form of protection, enabling the grower to provide near-ideal conditions for the crop. It gives better returns and allows greater control of the plant for certain crops, for example, tomatoes.

Each type of protection has its own characteristics and needs to be treated differently. Glass retains radiant heat whereas polyethylene does not, but poly-tunnels have a higher humidity. Modern developments in poly-tunnel design and construction now allow ridge ventilation but remove some of the main advantage of polyethylene, that is, cost. All types of protective structure have a part of play on the modern market garden and will be considered in turn.

GREENHOUSES

The modern trend in commercial greenhouse design is toward the Venlo type. This is a greenhouse that can be constructed in a variety of materials but has bays 10.5 feet wide. The eave height is normally 8.5 feet and can be varied to suit individual needs. The number of bays can be almost infinite, and additions can be added to these houses at a later date.

Most modern greenhouses are built around a steel structure and use aluminum glazing bars. The older types can have a steel frame and wooden glazing bars.

Greenhouses are expensive and can be bought either new or secondhand. There are some firms in this country that specialize in secondhand Dutch glass that is competitively priced and may work

Functional greenhouses can be more than a center of profit, but a beautiful addition to any operation.

out more cheaply than some of the more complex polyethylene tunnels.

When considering what type of greenhouse to buy, several factors need to be considered. Ventilation is important. Many greenhouses do not have adequate ventilation. Ideally, ventilators should be situated in the ridge of each bay, and both sides of the ridge should have openings. The total area of ventilators should approximate one-third of the floor area; in practice, this area is often reduced to one-sixth.

Another important consideration is light transmission. This may well relate to the use to which the greenhouse is to be put. Where crops are to be grown in winter when low light levels occur, any loss of available light will considerably reduce crop growth. For this reason, I would recommend the use of steel-framed houses with aluminum glazing bars. There is less structure in these types to shade the crop. When growing winter crops in wooden houses, painting the structure white will give more reflected light. Orientation of the greenhouse can also play a major part in light transmission. When the grower's main criterion is maximum winter light, the house should be oriented in such a way that the ridge casts the least shadow over the

A modern, aluminum-framed, Venlo-type greenhouse can be as easy as a two-day project.

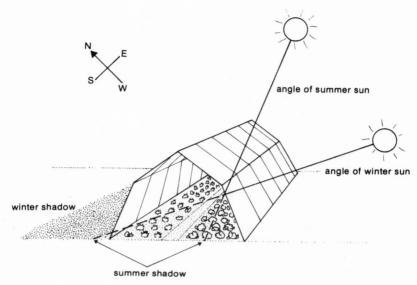

Figure 7.1. The shadow cast by a greenhouse in winter and summer.

crop. This will not be possible for large, multibay units.

The crops to be grown in a greenhouse will play a major part in deciding what type of structure is best. A tall, trained crop (tomatoes and cucumbers) will need good height and substantial crop supports. The ends of the greenhouse need to be well braced to prevent distortion.

A heating system of some sort may be desirable. There are a range of types that use a multitude of fuels. In small areas either gas or oil fired, free standing or suspended direct air heaters are the most common. Some form of heating will be necessary if out-of-season crops are to be grown. As a guide, a greenhouse should maintain a temperature approximately 4°F higher than outside, the glass trapping the radiant heat within the structure. When older greenhouses are used, regular maintenance of vents and glass fittings will ensure that no heat is lost through gaps. The side walls of structures can be insulated by using "bubble plastic," which may be let up in summer. The main disadvantage of this type of insulation is that it will reduce the amount of light entering the greenhouse. This may be improved by insulating the north side only. Wind can also dramatically reduce the amount of heat being retained. When positioning a greenhouse, a protected site should be selected or some form of windbreak should be positioned near the greenhouse.

Any greenhouse or poly-tunnel will need an irrigation system. Some form of overhead system of spraylines should be installed. These may use either aluminum pipes, which are expensive, or plastic, which tend to sag in the summer heat. In all cases, the nozzles should be arranged to

Bubble plastic insulation is often a real advantage in greenhouse operations. In this case it is being used on a cut flower crop (Alstroemeria).

prevent dripping onto the crop beneath. The spraylines should not be level to allow surplus water to drain down. This drain-down water needs to be piped outside or wet areas will be formed in the border soil.

All valves should be readily accessible. Lever valves—those that turn off quickly, unless you like a cold shower—are recommended. I also like to incorporate a hose point in each house, and the possibility of linking in a dilutor to enable liquid feeds to be applied should not be overlooked.

Do not forget access. One greenhouse I inherited on my own holding only had doors at one end, and it was 120 feet long. Tractors and equipment sometimes require more space to enter the greenhouse than expected.

Some provision should certainly be made to eliminate water being trapped on the greenhouse roof. Roof water should be drained away, ideally to a reservoir.

POLY-TUNNELS

In this section walk-in tunnels will be considered. These range in size from 14 feet in width upward. They can be obtained in lengths of up to 150 feet and may be single- or multispan. They are considerably cheaper than greenhouses.

The polyethylene skin will need replacing at regular intervals, usually every third season. When comparing various makes, the quality of the framework should be looked at in detail.

The smaller tunnels are relatively simple to erect, the ground tubes being hammered into the soil and then the steel work erected. The polyethylene is attached to a wooden end frame and then buried in a trench down the sides. When erecting the larger sizes more care is needed. Choose a calm day for covering—a sheet of polyethylene 150 feet by 40 feet takes some holding down. Even small covers can be impossible if there is any breeze.

As a growing environment, the poly-tunnel differs greatly from the greenhouse. Due to the construction, ventilation can be poor, particularly in the larger tunnels. The use of fans to aid air flow may be necessary. Siting a tunnel on a slight slope will improve air movement, with hot air rising and cold air draining to the low end. Condensation on the cover can be problematic, though some modern films are reported to reduce this problem. When high humidity levels and a lack of ventilation are combined, real problems can occur.

A typical walk-in poly-tunnel is inexpensive and a solution for many gardeners.

Ventilation in a poly-tunnel is critical—note the ventilator above the door.

The other major differences between polyethylene and glass is that of heat retention. Polyethylene, unlike glass, does not trap radiated heat. This means that at night the temperature in the tunnel will approximate the outside. The cover of a polyethylene tunnel will reduce the wind-chill factor and keep the crop warmer. There are, however, certain circumstances when temperatures can be lower inside a tunnel. Air movement or wind can, on some nights, prevent a frost from occurring. The tunnel protects the crop from wind and can actually encourage a frost. It may be possible to prevent this by opening up the vents (doors, etc.) to allow air movement.

A careful assessment of potential loadings on the frame is required when erecting crop supports. It may be best to erect a separate system of supports.

Poly-tunnels can be heated by similar systems to those mentioned in the section on greenhouses (see page 111). Double-skinned tunnels will reduce heat loss and condensation. The two layers of polyethylene will reduce the light levels. Irrigation will be needed, and the same systems that are available for a greenhouse are suitable under polyethylene. You must ensure that the water reaches all parts of the floor.

Spraylines in poly-tunnels can be aligned in a number of configurations. Note the hose at the end to remove the "drain down" water in this tunnel.

While talking of water, roof runoff must be considered. It is much more difficult to collect than that off a greenhouse, except for multispans. If several single-span tunnels are erected close to each other, drainage may be a real problem, particularly on sloping sites.

A wide range of crops can be grown successfully under polyethylene, within the limitations we have explored. Poly-tunnels have become popular due to the lower costs involved. For the same amount of capital investment, it is possible to erect double the amount of protective cover by opting for polyethylene as opposed to glass.

LOW POLYETHYLENE TUNNELS

These may be equated more accurately to polyethylene cloches. These can readily be made up on the market garden. They are cheap, easy to use and will advance growth. They can be used to cover a wide range of crops usually grown outside. Low polyethylene tunnels have

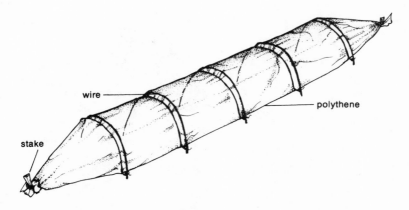

Figure 7.2. Low poly-tunnel or cloche.

been used with success on strawberries, lettuces, French beans, early marrows and courgettes. In fact, this method works on most low-growing crops. These tunnels are usually three feet wide and consist of a series of wire loops over which the polyethylene is laid. The polyethylene sheet is secured at each end by a stake and strings hold the polyethylene down to the hoops.

Ventilating such tunnels is easy. The polyethylene can be lifted on one or both sides and covered again at night. No special irrigation is required. Water will work its way in from the sides. Due to their construction, the application of crop protection chemicals can be time-consuming and weeding has to be done by hand. The covers may be used several times and the hoops should last for years.

There is a simple method for making the hoops. For a tunnel to cover a space approximately three feet wide, you will need:

    1.   A roll of polyethylene four feet wide.
    2.   A plank approximately six feet long.
    3.   Two large bolts of cotton reels.
    4.   A roll of stout wire.
    5.   Wire cutters.
    6.   Staples.

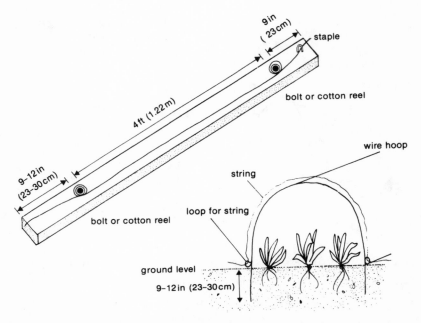

Figure 7.3. Board for making up hoop for low poly-tunnels, and hoop erected.

The plank should be set up as in Figure 7.3. The end of the wire is inserted in the staple. The wire is then wound once round the first bolt, taken straight across to the second bolt and wound around that and finally cut off at the end of the plank. The finished hoop should look like the one illustrated in Figure 7.3.

When erecting the hoops, ensure the string loops are on the outside. For added security a string can be tied from one end to the other and attached to the top of each hoop. Two hoops should be used at each end to prevent a collapse.

FLOATING FILMS

This is the latest development in protective cropping. The technique and the range of films have developed over the last five or so years, and now large areas are covered using this technique. Simply,

Floating film. perforated polyethylene type, is yet another idea in crop protection.

it is a large sheet of polyethylene or other material laid directly over the soil or young crop. Due to the protection and soil-warming properties, the crop will become established and grow faster than it would uncovered. This can improve the returns for that part of the crop and ease the spread of harvesting, and it has been claimed that some types of film exclude aphids.

There are now two basic types of film. The first is a perforated polyethylene sheet; the second is a sort of loosely woven material not unlike disposable diaper liners. Both types allow some air movement, which is important in preventing the buildup of high temperatures and reduces humidity levels. Water from rain or irrigation can also pass through both types of film.

The films can be laid by hand or machine and come in a range of widths, the narrower ones commonly being machine laid. Once down they are surprisingly secure because the wind tends to push them against the ground, unless an edge lifts and the wind can get underneath.

If the sheets are being used to cover a crop after sowing, the drills should be sunk into the seedbed to protect the emerging seedling

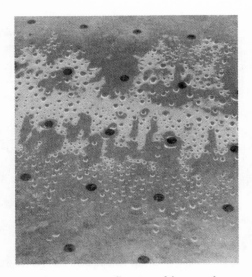

Condensation on floating film can be an advantage for reducing watering needs, but must be monitored for development of molds.

from damage. As the crop grows, the sheet is lifted. The outer row will suffer more damage than the inner rows and may in fact never reach a harvestable quality. For this reason, the use of wide sheets will reduce the proportion of outside rows.

The one critical operation when using floating films is to time their removal correctly. It is likely that more damage can be done by removing the film too late than too early. The time of harvest can be brought forward by up to two weeks by using these floating films. The lifting operation should be done with care so none of the sheet is left in the ground. It may be possible to reuse the sheet of film if damage has been kept to a minimum.

One drawback is that it is difficult to apply crop protection chemicals once the sheet is in place, so all possible spraying operations should be done before laying the film. It is not unknown for the film to be lifted to allow spraying and then replaced.

SUMMARY

Each of these four types of protection has its place in the modern market garden. They all work well within their own limitations and I used all four types on my own seven-acre market garden.

CHAPTER 8

Pest, Disease
and Weed Control

 *I*n this chapter the principles of pest, disease and weed control will be discussed. Some specific pests and diseases have been mentioned, with some indication of control measures, in Chapter 5. It is not possible to cover the full range of problems for the wide range of crops discussed in this book. It is, however, well worth considering the basic principles of pest and disease control, many of which make up what can only be described as good husbandry.

The primary aim of any grower must be to produce the crops required in such a way as to reduce to a minimum the likelihood of pest and disease infestation. This is made more difficult by the fact that crops will be grown intensively. The greater the numbers of an individual crop grown, the greater are the chances of a problem specific to that crop occurring.

For the sake of simplicity, this subject of pest and disease control will be divided into two sections, namely preventative measures and control measures.

PREVENTATIVE MEASURES

In this section we will consider good husbandry techniques.

First and foremost, the grower's aim must be to produce a healthy plant. To do this, the plant requires its own ideal environmental conditions. The nature of the soil in which it is growing is of vital importance, as discussed in Chapter 3. Providing the crop with a soil of good, balanced nutrient status, with a good structure and no problems of impeded drainage and compaction, will enable the plant to be healthy. A healthy plant, like a healthy person, is more able to fight off pest and disease attacks using its own resources. This is a point of view that has been argued quite strongly by the modern organic movement and has tended to be overlooked by the rest of the horticultural community. The modern market gardener asks a lot of his basic resource, the soil. He or she takes a lot out and needs to put a lot in to maintain the natural balance.

One way this balance can be helped is by working a good rotation. The use of rotation will do two things: It will help balance the demands on the soil by the crops and also help prevent the buildup of soil-borne pathogens. When considering this latter point, the longer the time interval between similar crops the better. The one real problem with rotations is that for reasons of economics and marketing opportunity, the grower may have decided on a cropping schedule that involves specialization in certain crops. I would recommend that, if at all possible, some form of rotation be practiced. It may be that certain areas can be left fallow or a green manure crop can be grown on areas not actively being cropped. When this is not possible the grower should, at the least, be aware of the possible pitfalls.

After rotation and the soil, the general growing conditions need to be considered. It is not possible to change the other environmental conditions under which the crop is grown except by the use of protective structures (as discussed in Chapter 7). To help reduce the incidence of pathogen infection in these areas, the grower should ensure the conditions are such that they do not encourage the buildup of the pathogens. This can be done by ensuring that there is adequate ventilation and air movement through the crop. Such techniques as watering early in the day so the crop canopy (leaves) dries out before nightfall will help.

When carrying out any cultural operations, such as weed control or training, every effort should be made to keep any damage to the crop to a minimum. This may seem like common sense, but while a broken leaf may not reduce the quality of the crop, it offers an easy entry point for disease.

A crop that has been grown "soft" is more tempting to sap-

Good hygiene around the market garden is the first consideration in controlling pests and disease.

sucking insects, such as aphids. Infestations may be reduced by growing the crop with a "harder" regime. While on the subject of aphids, there has in the past been a move to eradicate the pests' winter host. Latest research shows that removal of the spindletree (*Euonymus europeus*) from the hedgerows does not reduce the incidence of black bean aphid in broad beans. Keeping a variety of flora and fauna on the uncropped areas of the holding will encourage the presence of natural predators in the area and help the grower's efforts to control pests. Encouraging ladybugs is the classic example.

Next on the list of preventative measures is hygiene. Put simply, hygiene is the elimination of any potential source of infection. The most obvious source is crop debris left after harvest. This should not be allowed to remain for any length of time. Depending on what problems the previous crop has encountered, it may be sufficient to incorporate it quickly into the soil. If the debris is removed from the growing area, it should not be dumped close to other similar crops. All rubbish areas should be regularly maintained to prevent fungal spores being carried onto healthy crops. This can be done by composting the organic matter or covering it with soil. In some cases burning may be necessary.

Water sources should also be protected from infection where possible. That ideal site for a rubbish dump by the reservoir may not be so ideal after all.

All machinery and equipment should be cleaned regularly. This is particularly important if it has been working on or in an infected soil. In fact, soil-borne diseases, such as clubroot, have been known to move from one holding to another on tractor wheels or even on boots of visitors. I don't mean to advocate a policy of isolation, but prevention is cheaper than cure.

All propagating materials should be regularly sterilized as should the structure of any greenhouse or poly-tunnel. In intensively cropped areas, it can be beneficial to sterilize the soil as a routine preventative measure. Chemicals or steam sterilization can be used. Steam is becoming a possibility again with the innovation of small, portable steam generators.

Finally, with regard to hygiene, do not overlook the work force and tools, such as knives. Several tomato diseases can be spread by infected knives or fingers.

The use of clean seed and plant material can go a long way in preventing the introduction of any pests and diseases. All seed suppliers offer a range of treatments on their seeds. While increasing the cost of the seed initially, it may be the cheapest measure of controlling certain diseases. This avenue is not open to the organic grower and most seed houses now supply a range of untreated varieties available. If in doubt about seed treatments, a chat with the local seed salesman will be worthwhile. In many respects the same is true of plant suppliers. Some spray their plants as a matter of course; others do not. If you have specific requirements, chat with the suppliers and find out. While it is in the interest of the plant supplier to send out only clean plants, this does not always happen, and any plants brought in should be inspected closely at the time of delivery.

When choosing what variety of plant to grow it can be beneficial to choose one that is resistant to certain pests and diseases. I have already mentioned the parsnip Avon Reister (see Chapter 5, page 76). Most modern tomato varieties are TMV resistant or green-back resistant. Many varieties of lettuce are resistant to certain strains of mildew. By careful selection of resistant varieties many problems can be eliminated. Plant breeders are working all the time to improve this natural form of prevention so keep up-to-date and some problems can be prevented.

Finally, as far as preventative measures go, it may be necessary to take drastic action to prevent the occurrence of outbreaks of certain pests and diseases. This may mean not growing the crop at all, or possibly growing in an isolated medium, such as peat modules or grow bags. Normally, this is only practiced where a specific soil problem has become uncontrollable or if the grower needs to be able to control the plant more precisely.

CONTROL MEASURES

It is likely that no matter how careful a grower is with preventative measures, he or she will suffer some, if not many, pathogen infestations. When this occurs some form of curative measure needs to be taken.

There are three basic ways the problems can be attacked:
1. Chemical pesticides.
2. Biological means.
3. An integrated system combining both 1 and 2 above.

Before we look at each of these in turn, the grower needs to know when to instigate a method of control. In most cases the problem can be controlled more easily if the symptoms are seen soon enough. To be sure of doing this, all crops should be regularly inspected. In fact, this can be a relaxing and worthwhile job. Walking through the crops as regularly as possible, inspecting for pathogen attack and noting crop growth and development, enables the grower to keep on top of problems. This is preferable to waiting for a problem to develop and then trying to solve it. Staff should be instructed to look for anything unusual, even to the extent of offering a reward for the first whitefly!

Chemical Pesticides

Control of pathogen attack by means of chemicals is by far the most common method. It is not the intention of this section to recommend specific chemicals for problems. For this, contact the local extension office, consult relevant publications or talk to a local supplier.

Before going any further, we need to be aware of the recent changes in the law concerning the application of pesticides. There has been a number of regulations enacted over the last few years regarding the use of pesticides. For the grower, these regulations basically mean the following:

Pathways should allow access to all parts of the crop when spraying (lettuce seedlings).

1. Chemicals can only be used in approved circumstances; the details should be on the product label.
2. Anyone applying such chemicals should follow all application guidelines for the specific method of application being used.

For further information and for advice, contact your local cooperative extension service office or state department of agriculture. These regulations are designed to protect the grower, his or her staff, the public and the environment.

When deciding how best to apply chemicals, thought should be given to how to get the chemical where it will be effective. Many pests live on the undersides of leaves and spray droplets need to be directed here. Fine sprays will enable maximum amounts of chemical to be absorbed by the plant. Therefore, droplet size will play an important part in successful application. All equipment used should be well maintained and calibrated (see Chapter 6, page 100).

Chemical use can be a successful control to both pests and disease, but safety for everyone involved is the number one consideration in selection and use.

When using chemicals to control both pests and diseases, a range of different chemicals should be used. This prevents the buildup of resistant strains of pathogens. Strains of lettuce mildew have developed resistance to Metalaxyl, and some pests are resistant to certain insecticides. By ringing the changes, this can be prevented. The chemical should be changed each time the crop is sprayed, and it is usual practice to have a minimum of three different chemicals in the spray program. This is true for both insecticides and fungicides.

Pathogen control does not stop with harvest. It is sensible to fumigate all crop debris before removal from protective structures as moving crop rubbish will disperse fungal spores and insects. Do not forget rubbish dumps as well. Regular fumigation and sterilization of the physical structure of greenhouses and tunnels should be carried out to prevent pests and diseases overwintering and infecting future crops. I used commercial formaldehyde and appropriate protective clothing for this. The soil will need attention, too.

When using chemicals, it goes without saying that all harvest intervals must be strictly adhered to. The time of application is also important. All spraying operations should be carried out in cool weather. This helps to prevent any damage to the crop from scorch. The best time is in the evening when insects are often still active and the temperature has dropped. It allows the plant to absorb the maximum amount of chemical and none is lost by volatilization.

Chemical control can be effective, and it provides the grower with a wide range of weapons to protect crops and ensure an economic return for the grower's labors.

Biological Control

At present, the range of pests that can be controlled biologically is limited. Research is continuing to find new methods. The pests for which biological control is currently available include red spider mites, whiteflies, leaf miners, mealy bugs, caterpillars and some aphids.

How does biological control work? The pest is controlled by introducing a predator or parasite that is specific to that pest. This

Tagetes used to discourage insects is an effective control system.

predator or parasite then kills off the pest. In practice, this means that the pest can be kept to acceptable levels. It is possible to eradicate the pest, but as we shall see, this may not be desirable. Before progressing any further, it should be said that biological control works best indoors or with polyethylene. The predators tend to prefer higher temperatures than can normally be expected outdoors in many parts of the United States, but they can still be effective there.

Biological control can be used in two ways. The aim of the first system is to prevent a buildup of the pest over the growing season of the crop. This is done by introducing the pest and predator at an early stage in the crop growth. The number of predators will control the pest to acceptable levels. If a sudden infestation occurs from outside sources, the predator is ready to multiply to deal with it. In severe attacks, a further introduction of predator may be necessary to achieve control quickly. When using this system, regular monitoring of both pest and predator is needed to ensure that the predator is always present.

The second system is a relatively short-term control. Introduction of the predator is left until the pest has infected the crop. The rate of introduction of the predator is related to the level of infestation, and

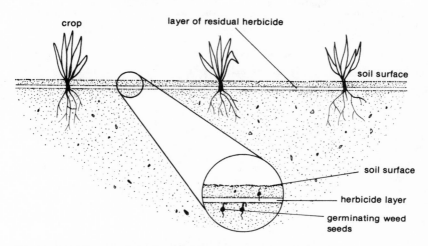

Figure 8.1. Layer of residual herbicide in damp soil.

rapid control is possible. I have used this method with success when an infestation of red spider mite on a cold tomato crop took place in August.

These control methods apply where the insect predator or parasite is used to control the pest, that is, the red spider mite, whitefly and leaf miner. It can be applied either as routine sprays or in response to damage. The aphid control *Verticillium lecanii* is a fungus and is applied the same way. When applying sprays of these two controls, high-volume sprays should be used to ensure a thorough wetting of the plants.

Other means of biological control can be used. Colored boards smeared with a sticky substance such as petroleum jelly can be suspended above the crop. Bright yellow is the color most insects find attractive; they fly to the board and become stuck to it. These boards are good indicators of a pest infestation and can be used as an early warning system.

Many pests are attracted to the plant by smell, for example carrot- and cabbage-root flies. It may be possible to mask the smell of the crop. Research is underway to establish if it is possible to use this mechanism for pest control. Companion planting often works in this way. The planting of marigolds near crops affected by aphid and whitefly can be useful. The smell is strong and masks the scent of the normal host plant, so the aphid and whitefly are not attracted to it. People are put off by strong smells, and insects are more sensitive to odor than we are!

As we have seen, biological means for control of pathogens is effective, but limited. It has advantages over chemical control in that there is no harvest interval, no damage to crops and less time—if any— is spent spraying. Also, it cannot pollute or damage the environment or be harmful to staff or customers.

Integrated Control

This system utilizes both biological and chemical control and so combines these two methods. Its use is becoming more widespread as the common pests can be controlled biologically, but chemicals are used where no biological control is possible. In this system, careful selection of the chemicals is vital as many will adversely affect the predator. The best advice on what chemicals can be used safely can be obtained from the suppliers of biological control agents.

Weed Control

As with pest control, weeds can be controlled both by chemical and natural means. (By natural, I mean mechanical.) Weed control equipment was covered in Chapter 6, page 98. Suffice it to say that there is a wide range of mechanical weeders available.

When considering chemical weed control we need to ascertain the mode of action of these herbicides.

Contact Herbicides—As the name implies, these kill on contact. The exact mode of action varies slightly, but basically the chemical will kill that part it touches. Paraquat is a good example. It will not kill the roots of plants such as dock or thistle and is totally nonselective in action. It will kill weed and crop, grass and broadleaf alike.

Polyethylene mulch used for weed control can be utilized at limited expense. Strawberries do very well in this environment.

Translocated Herbicides—In this group, the active ingredient is absorbed by the plant and transferred to all parts. This has the great advantage that the roots will be killed as well as the aerial parts.

Residual Herbicides—These are so called because the residues stay in the soil, and they can work in a variety of ways. They may prevent germination of weed seedlings. The chemical can be absorbed by the roots of young weeds and hence kill them. Some residual herbicides also have contact action. With these residual herbicides not all weeds may be controlled by the chemical. Care is needed in selecting the right herbicide. Take the following into account:

1. The weed species that are the problem (weed spectrum).
2. The crop plant; it may also be susceptible.
3. The soil type and moisture content.

This latter point is important when it comes to applying the chemical. Soil-acting herbicides are spread in moist soil and form a layer just below the surface. This will not occur if the soil surface is too rough or too dry. Once a soil-acting herbicide is applied, the ground should not be disturbed. It is possible to apply such chemicals after planting, but when doing so take care to ensure that the correct dose is applied or crop damage will result.

Selective Herbicides—These may be one of the above types. They are called selective because they only kill certain kinds of plants and will leave the crop undamaged. Hormone herbicides can be classified as selective, as they do not work on grasses or cereals but kill broad-leafed plants. Tomatoes are sensitive to hormone herbicides and damage can easily occur from spray drift.

Total Herbicides—These kill all plants and should only be used in extreme cases as the chemical can remain in the soil for several seasons.

There are other forms of weed control. Mulches can be used; these may consist of polyethylene, special paper, straw, etc. The idea of mulching is to cover the soil surface with a layer of sterile medium. It can act as a physical barrier, such as black polyethylene, or just be too deep for weeds to push their way through, such as straw. Mulches also have the advantage of retaining moisture and can help improve soil temperatures. Weeds can also be suppressed by the use of a low-growing green manure crop such as clover. This will protect the soil from damage, can be incorporated after cropping and can generally help fertility.

Effective pest, disease and weed control will be a combination of many factors. Good general husbandry, a fertile soil, good hygiene and careful selection of varieties will help to prevent infestations. When these do occur, a range of options is open to the grower. Under protected structures the use of biological means, either on their own, or integrated with chemicals, can be effective and have advantages. Chemicals themselves can be extremely effective.

No one system is foolproof, and the grower must adopt that which is best suited to his or her own methods and preferences. There are a great many potential problems from pests, diseases and weeds, but thankfully, usually only a handful occur each season. It is not often a crop is a total loss thanks to the modern methods of control available today.

CHAPTER 9

Management

*T*o run a successful enterprise the owner or manager has to have a wide range of abilities. We all have a flair for particular things, and any skills that are needed can usually be bought. In many respects, financial advice is one of the easiest things to buy. A desire to succeed, combined with enthusiasm and an ability to learn, will go a long way.

The grower should pay attention to detail in all aspects of the business. Most people who like getting their hands dirty do not like the paperwork, but it needs to be done. Keeping up-to-date records so you can see where you are financially is just as important as being on top of the growing side. All this may sound a bit daunting but don't let it put you off. It certainly will not be easy. It will involve long hours and the financial rewards may not always be good, but there is a satisfaction in producing good crops and seeing the results of your labors that is like no other.

RESOURCES

Making the most of all available resources really sums up a manager's ability. In Chapter 3 we looked at managing that prime resource, the soil. Marketing possibilities have also been discussed. In Chapter 6 on mechanization, financial implications were raised. All these, plus the manager's own ability, and that of the staff, must be added together to produce an efficient, well-run, profitable organization. To make the most of that unique blend, each of the resources must be appraised. When the marketing opportunities, soil type and site are considered any decision regarding cropping may be made.

The manager's own abilities and those of the staff can be

improved by training in the areas of weakness, so there should not really be a problem here.

The other major hurdle to overcome is financial. To make the most of what financing is available, plans should be drawn up.

PLANNING

It is surprising how many successful holdings have just grown haphazardly. Life can be made much easier with careful planning. By this, I mean all types of planning.

A cropping plan needs to be made out for each season. Records should be kept so it can be modified in future to gain maximum advantage. Cropping plans rarely work out in practice due to nature's ability to complicate the best laid plans. If you do have an organized plan, the effects of a delayed crop can be seen and assessed early. It may indicate that changes should be made later in the season, and planning for these changes now can turn them to an advantage.

Access and parking at a farm shop is part of the basic plan when considering on-farm marketing.

Consistently appearing at the same place at the same time in a flea market or farmers market helps establish a customer base for your produce.

A development plan for the holding is also extremely useful and should cover a number of years: the following year in detail, provisional plans for the next four or five years and a long-term plan for ten or more years hence. This prevents expensive mistakes, such as installing structures or irrigation mains where they will not be needed in the future.

These long-term plans of physical resources should be linked in with financial plans. If you are borrowing money, your bank will need to know your plans anyway, so projecting into the future should not be difficult.

While on the subject of planning, we should consider local authority planning regulations. Planning laws vary around the country, and permission may or may not be required for the erection of greenhouses, packing sheds, poly-tunnels and the like. Even composting may fall under zoning regulations.

If you are considering opening a farm shop, it is often the case that planning consent is not required if you sell only your own produce. Rates may be affected as well if a retail outlet is envisaged. If you are in any doubt about local regulations contact the local authority concerned.

When considering retail outlets on the holding, access to and from the road must be considered. What might be acceptable for your own driveway may not be acceptable for access by the general public. The highway department of your county or state can help.

When a plan is produced it enables the manager to develop a basic strategy to achieve the goals by utilizing the resources available. It can be modified in the light of experience and varying circumstances; the goals may change but with careful planning should still be within reach.

FINANCE

In the previous section financial planning was mentioned, but it is also necessary to keep financial records. For one thing, both state and federal revenue services require certain records and all financial details to be kept. The manager, to be effective, needs to know exactly where his or her business stands at any one time. The annual balance sheets, prepared some months after the end of the financial year, are not enough on which to base sound financial judgment. The manager will be making decisions all the time, and the more information he or she has the more logical will be his or her decisions.

It is possible to formulate a relatively simple system of bookkeeping that will keep both the Internal Revenue Service and your state revenue department happy and still provide the financial information the manager requires. In fact, modern desktop computers can be an asset; software packages are available for cropping details, etc. If you are happy using a computer, it has advantages. If you prefer not to use a computer, stick to your own system. Whatever method is adopted, it should be easy and convenient. If this is so, it is much more likely to be kept up-to-date.

While on the subject of finance, we cannot ignore the fact that most businesses use borrowed money at some stage. It may be for capital investment or for working capital to tide one over during the quiet period. One word of caution: Do not overborrow. The returns from growing are not the greatest, and interest rates vary. The ability to repay the loan and pay for living expenses needs to be looked at carefully.

Banks are the most usual source of finance but not the only ones. This whole subject of finance and financial management is a complex one. There are books and courses available to help the grower gain a greater understanding and develop skills in this area.

INSURANCE

Insurance is available to cover a wide range of risks. Public liability and employer's liability are both likely to be necessary. Some structures may be insurable against a range of risks. Polyethylene tunnels are one area that can be difficult. Normally, it is possible to insure the framework but not the cover. Greenhouses can be insured and when insuring them, be sure to include coverage to pay for removal of glass from the site. In the event of major damage, it can take many man-hours to remove all the broken glass. Crops can be covered for certain risks. It may be possible to insure greenhouse crops against heating system breakdowns, etc., but it will be expensive. What may be cheaper is to insure against potential loss of income, though outdoor crops are not usually insurable. It goes without saying that all vehicles and equipment should be covered.

TRAINING

This, perhaps, seems an unusual section to include in a chapter on management, and I have already mentioned it several times. Great improvements can be made in the business by identifying where there are skill shortages and rectifying these shortages thorough good training programs.

Good gardening skills are not enough to run a successful market garden enterprise. Good management and sales skills are just as important.

At the start of this chapter I suggested that a grower should have a wide range of skills. Very few people will be good at all aspects of running a market garden. Once the areas of weakness have been identified, try to find a training course to help develop skills in these particular areas.

There are two main sources of training throughout the country. These are the courses offered through garden societies, associations and the cooperative extension service or more structured courses offered through agricultural colleges. There are grower groups and associations that may run their own training courses as well. Most of these can be found in the yellow pages under "Training." They all run a vast range of courses from basic horticultural skills up to longer management courses. The extension specialists may be able to help develop a complete training program for the individual business. Most courses are organized during the period from October to March, when life tends to be a little quieter.

Running a successful business depends on many things, as we have seen. It is not possible in a book such as this to cover all aspects in detail. The owner/manager will have a wide range of skills already, and it is relatively easy to gain new ones by attending any of the excellent training courses being offered today. Careful planning and attention to detail combined with optimism and enthusiasm will get you by. There is nothing quite as satisfying as growing. Good luck.

Liming Materials

Calcium Carbonate—Soft chalk, limestone.

Most common liming material, cheap and safe, readily available.

Calcium Oxide—Quicklime, burnt lime, cob lime or caustic lime.

Not used much. It burns and is a fire risk.

Calcium Hydroxide—Hydrated lime or slaked lime.

Fine white powder. Commonly used in composts. High neutralizing value. Works relatively quickly.

Magnesian Lime—Dolomitic limestone.

Used in composts and under glass as it includes magnesium, but it acts slowly.

U.S. Measure and Metric Measure Conversion Chart

When You Know:	Multiply By:	Conversion To:
MASS		
ounces (oz.)	28.35	grams
pounds (lb.)	0.45	kilograms
grams (g.)	0.035	ounces
kilograms (kg.)	2.2	pounds
VOLUME		
pints (pt.)	0.47	liters
quarts (qt.)	0.95	liters
gallons (gal.)	3.785	liters
milliliters (ml.)	0.034	fluid ounces
LENGTH		
inches (in.)	2.54	centimeters
feet (ft.)	30.48	centimeters
yards (yd.)	0.9144	meters
miles (mi.)	1.609	kilometers
kilometers (km.)	0.621	miles
meters (m.)	1.094	yards
centimeters (cm.)	0.39	inches
TEMPERATURE		
Fahrenheit (°F)	5/9 (subtracting 32)	Celsius
Celsius (°C)	9/5 (then add 32)	Fahrenheit

AREA

square inches (in.^{2})	6.452	square centimeters
square feet (ft.^{2})	929.0	square centimeters
square yards (yd.^{2})	8361.0	square centimeters
acres (a.)	0.4047	hectares

Associations

All-American Selections National Garden Bureau, Inc., 1311 Butterfield Road, Suite 310, Downers Grove, IL 60515, (708) 963-0770. Tests new varieties of vegetables and flowers grown from seed, has test gardens located all over the United States. Write for list.

American Association of Nurserymen, 1250 I Street, #500, Washington, D.C. 20005, (202) 789-2900. Trade association providing services and information to nurserymen.

American Herb Association, P.O. Box 353, Rescue, CA 95672. Publishes sources and directories for herb gardeners.

American Horticultural Society, 7931 E. Boulevard Drive, Alexandria, VA 22308, (703) 768-5700. A gardener's information service.

American Seed Trade Association, 1030 15th Street N.E., Suite 964, Washington, D.C. 20005, (202) 223-4080. Trade association of seed companies. Write for information.

Association of Specialty Cut Flower Growers, 155 Elm Street, Oberlin, OH 44074, (216) 774-2887. Group dedicated to growing cut flowers for market.

Bio-Dynamic Farming and Gardening Association, P.O. Box 550, Kimberton, PA 19442, (215) 935-7797. Promotes the bio-dynamic method of farming and gardening.

Bio-Integral Resource Center, P.O. Box 7414, Berkeley, CA 94707, (415) 524-2567. Group devoted to the least toxic methods of pest management.

Canadian Organic Growers, P.O. Box 6408, Station J, Ottawa, Ontario, Canada K2A 3Y6.

The Croft Institute, Rt. 3, Box 73, Stanley, WI 54768, (715) 644-

2499. Organization devoted to promoting small-scale organic food production for home and market gardeners.

The Fertilizer Institute, 1015 18th Street N.W., Washington, D.C. 20036, (202) 861-4934, (202) 789-2900. Trade association. Write for information.

Herb Research Foundation, P.O. Box 2602, Longmont, CO 80501, (303) 449-2265. Research group dedicated to herbs.

Horticultural Research Institute, 1250 I Street N.W., Suite 500, Washington, D.C. 20005, (202) 789-2900. Trade association associated with American Association of Nurserymen.

International Herb Growers and Marketers Association, P.O. Box 281, Silver Springs, PA 17575, (717) 285-4252. Group of producers and marketers dedicated to herbs and to educating the public about herbs and herb-related products.

National Gardening Association, Member Subscription Service, Depot Square, Peterborough, NH 03458, (802) 863-1308. Dedicated to teaching people how to grow food.

National Xeriscape Council, Inc., 940 East 51st Street, Austin, TX 78751, (512) 454-8626. Nonprofit group devoted to "xeriscaping." Write for information.

Outdoor Power Equipment Institute, 1901 L Street N.W., #700, Washington, D.C. 20036, (202) 296-3484. Trade association. Write for information.

Regenerative Agriculture Association, 222 Main Street, Emmaus, PA 18049, (215) 967-5171. Association of commercial farmers using organic methods.

Soil & Water Conservation Society, 7515 N.E. Ankeny Road, Ankeny, IA 50021, (515) 289-2331. Association dedicated to the advancement of the science and art of land use.

BIBLIOGRAPHY

Adams, C.R., D.D. Bamford, and M.P. Early. *Principles of Horticulture.* Portsmouth, NH: Heinemann, 1984.

Arden-Clarke, C., and P. Hodges. "Soil Erosion: The Answer Lies in Organic Farming." *New Scientist* (12 February 1987).

Bould, C., E.J. Hewitt, and P. Needham. *Diagnosis of Mineral Disorders in Plants, Vol. 1, Principles.* Norwich, England: HMSO, 1983.

Burr, Fearing. *Field and Garden Vegetables of America.* Chillicothe, IL: American Botanist, 1988.

Davies, B., D. Eagle, and B. Finney. *Soil Management.* Suffolk, England: Farming Press, second impression 1979.

Fletcher, J. T. *Diseases of Greenhouse Plants.* White Plains, NY: Longman, 1984.

Hill, Lewis. *Secrets of Plant Propagation.* Pownal, VT: Storey Communications, 1985.

Hunt, Marjorie B., and Brenda Bortz. *High-Yield Gardening: How to Get More From Your Garden Space and More From Your Garden Season.* Emmaus, PA: Rodale Press, 1986.

Kowalchik, C., and William H. Hylton, eds. *Rodale's Illustrated Encyclopedia of Herbs.* Emmaus, PA: Rodale Press, 1987.

Maddox, H. *Your Garden Soil.* Devon, England: David & Charles, 1974.

Robertson, J. *Mechanising Vegetable Production.* Suffolk, England: Farming Press, 1974.

Sarjent, M.J. *Economics in Horticulture.* New York: The Macmillan Press Ltd., 1973.

Webber, R. *Market Gardening.* Devon, England: David & Charles, 1972.

PERIODICALS

The Bu$iness of Herbs, Northwind Farm Publications, Rt. 2, Box 246, Shevlin, MN 56676.

Country Journal, Cowles Magazines, P.O. Box 392, Mt. Morris, IL 61054.

Gardeners Share, P.O. Box 243, Columbus, IN 47273.

The Growing Edge Magazine, P.O. Box 1027, Corvallis, OR 97339.

Harrowsmith, Camden House Publishing, Ferry Road, Charlotte, VT 05445.

The Herb Companion, Interweave Press, Inc., 306 N. Washington Avenue, Loveland, CO 80537.

The Herb Quarterly, Long Mountain Press, Inc., P.O.Box 548, Boiling Springs, PA 17007

Horticulture, Horticulture Limited Partnership, P.O. Box 2595, Boulder, CO 80323.

The IPM Practitioner, Bio-Integral Research Center, P.O. Box 7414, Berkeley, CA 94707.

Living Off the Land, Geraventure, P.O. Box 2131, Melbourne, FL 32902.

New Farm, Rodale Press, Inc., 33 East Minor Street, Emmaus, PA 18098.

Organic Gardening, Rodale Press, Inc., 33 East Minor Street, Emmaus, PA 18098.

Small Farm News, Small Farm Center, Cooperative Extension, University of California, Davis, CA 95616.

INDEX

acid rain 53
acidity 53
agents, marketing 19–20
alkalinity 52, 61
alterneria leafspot 64
anthracnose 70
aphids 66,131
    black bean 70
aubergines 86

beans 12, 66, 68–70
    broad 68
    brown 69
    French 68
    green 23
    pinched 68
    runner 68
bedding plants 91
bees 70
beetroot 76
beets 23, 72
biological control 4
bonemeal 49
boron 59
botrytis 86
brassicas 63–64
broccoli 62

cabbages 62, 64
    root fly 65, 133–134
calcium 52–53
canker 76
carrots 16, 23, 72, 74–75
    baby 75
    root fly 75, 76, 133–134
catering outlets 16
caterpillars 66, 86, 131
cauliflowers 63, 64
cavity spot 76
celeriac 77
celery 75, 80, 88–89
chemicals 25, 130 (*see also* infestation, pest and disease)
    regulations of 129
chickweed 76
Chinese leaves 16
chocolate spot 70
clay 31, 34, 35
clean-air policy 55
clovers 48
club root 62, 64
cold store 103–104
Colorado Organic Certification Act of 1989 9
companion planting 134
compost 34–35, 48
    loamless 49
computers 142
cooperatives 20–21
copper 59
courgettes 79
cucumbers 85
cultivation pan 37–38

cultivator, rotary 37, 93, 95 (*see also* Rototiller)
    tined 97

deficieny:
    nutrient 56–57
    trace element 58
development, stages of 71
diseases 64–66, 70, 71–72, 75–76, 77, 81, 85, 86, 88–89
display 23
downy mildew 71
drainage 37–38

eelworm 71
Epsom salts 51
Euonymus europeus (spindletree) 126

F1 hybrids 63
Farm Bill, 1990 4
farmers market 1, 13, 15
farm shop 1, 5, 11–12, 140, 142
farmyard manure 42, 43, 48, 53, 60, 66, 70, 81, 88
fennel 77
fertilizer 74
    spreaders 101
finances 139–140, 142–143
    loans 143
    records 142
    software 142
flea markets 14, 15, 141
floating film 7, 73, 74, 75, 122
fruit 2, 12, 23, 90–91
fusarium 85

ghost spotting 85

greenhouse 112, 113, 114, 115, 126, 141 (*see also* structures, protective)

grading, equipment 103–104

grants 21

green manure 42–48

halo blight 70

harvesting, equipment 103

hay 41

health ordinances 24

heating systems 114–115

herbicides 64, 133, 136

herbs 89–90

humus 34

hygiene 125, 126

infestation, pest and disease:

    control of 128

        biological 131–134

        chemical 128–131

        integrated 134

        weed 134

            herbicides 134, 136–137

insurance 143

Internal Revenue Service 142

iron 59

irrigation 76, 80, 83, 88

    equipment 105–109

    trickle 84

kieserite 51

kohlrabi 62, 77

ladybugs 126
leaf miners 131
leaf spot 64, 88–89
leeks 66, 68, 70–71
       moth 72
legislation, state 4
lettuce 79, 80
leys 48
light transmission 113–114
lime 52–53
       induced chlorosis 52–53
       materials 147
liquid feeds 85
location 10
lucerne 42
lupins 48

magnesium 51
magnesium sulfate 51 (*see also* kieserite)
manganese 55
markets:
       national 19–20
       regional 18–19
marketing 9–25, 139–140
marketing cooperative 103
marrows 77–79
mayweed 76
mealy bugs 131
measures, conversion chart 149–150
Metalaxyl 131
mildew 86, 87
molybdenum 59
monocropping 42–43
mulches 137

National Organic Standards Board (NOSB) 2, 4, 6
nematodes (*see* eelworm)
nitrates 46
nitrogen 45–48, 72
      cycle 47
nutrition, requirements for crops 45

Ocean Spray 19–20
onions 66, 68, 70–71
      fly 71
      salad 80
open pollination 63
organic:
      matter 34–35, 46, 66
      movement 4, 6
      pest control 65
      production 2
oxygen 46

packaging 19, 21, 23
panning 37, 97
pans cultivation 38
parsley 75
parsnips 72, 74–75
      Avon Reister 76, 127
peas 12, 66, 67
      sugar 68
      mange-tout 68
peppers 12, 16, 23, 86
pests 64–66, 70, 71–72, 75–76, 77, 81, 85, 86, 88–89, 130
petroleum jelly 133
pH 52–53, 66, 70, 72, 74, 81, 87
      meter 52

phosphorus (phosphaste) 48–49, 64, 72
    rock 49
    super 49
    triple 49
pick-your-own garden 1, 2, 12, 78
planning 140–142
    cropping plan 140
    development plan 141
    long-term plan 141
    regulations 140
plant spacing 63
plants, potted 91
plows 37, 97
polyethylene 80, 116, 118, 119, 121, 135
    (*see also* structures, protective)
    tunnels 7, 126, 141, 143
pore spaces 38
potash 64, 72
potassium (potash) 49, 50
potatoes 72, 76–77
    blight 77
    nematodes 77
    scab 77
    wire worm 77
precision drilling 76, 101
presentation, produce 22
pricing 24
pseudomonas 65
pumpkins 79

radishes 62, 80, 89
red spider mite 85, 86, 131
retailer, local 15–16

ring spot 64

rotation, crop 42–43

Rototiller 7, 38, 39, 93, 95, 96, 97–98, 100
   (*see also* cultivator, rotary)

rototilling 36

rust 72

sales tax 24

salsify 72

sand 30, 35

sclerotinia 88

scorzonera 72, 77

shrubs 91

silt 30, 35

slugs 88

soil:

   analysis 29–30

   classification 28

   compaction 38, 43, 74, 97

   crumb structure 34, 35, 97

   damage 37–38, 40

   erosion 42

   fertility 38

   management 35–43

   moisture content 38–40

   pores 37

   profile 31–33, 35, 46

   properties 28

   structure 33–35

   texture 33

   type 139

spacing 74

spices 16

spinach 66, 72

spindletree (*Euonymus europeus*) 126
sprayers 99–101, 106, 107, 129
sprinkler 105
sprouts 64
squash 79
staff 13
stale seedbed 64, 70
stands, roadside 6
sterilization steam 81, 126
straw 42, 74
strawberries 90, 136
structures, protective 80–83, 111–112
    access to 115
    floating films 120–122
    glass 111
    greenhouses 111–115
    low polyethylene tunnels 118–120
    poly-tunnels 81, 115, 116–118
subsoil 31–33
subsoilers 95, 97
sulphur 53, 55
swedes 62
sweet corn 12, 77, 78

tagetes 132
timing, soil cultivations 35
tolerance, of crops 54
tomatoes 23, 50, 83, 84–85, 86
    beef 84
    cherry 51
    plum 84
    yellow 84
topsoil 32
trace elements 55, 59–60

tractor 93, 94
training 143–145
transplants 70
transportation:
      off-holding 104
      on-holding 104
turnips 62

U.S. Department of Agriculture 2

vegetables 61–79
      brassicas 49, 62–66, 72
      legumes 66–72
      roots 72–79
ventilation 83
Verticillium lecanii 133
violet root rot 76

water rights 108
weed control:
      chemical 70, 77
      machinery 98–99
whitefly 85, 131
white rot 71
wholesalers, local 17–18

zinc 59

*R*ic Staines is a lecturer in commercial horticulture at Otley College in Suffolk, England, specializing in commercial vegetable and commercial organic production. Before his academic career, he owned and worked a seven-acre market garden. He became involved in the formation of a local marketing cooperative and eventually became a director of a large national marketing cooperative. He currently has a gardening program on BBC Radio.